BIG CATS

BIG CATS

Barbara Radcliffe Rogers

GALLERY BOOKS

An Imprint of W.H. Smith Publishers, Inc.

112 Madison Avenue

New York, New York 10016

A FRIEDMAN GROUP BOOK

This edition published in 1991 by GALLERY BOOKS
An imprint of W.H. Smith Publishers, Inc.
112 Madison Avenue
New York, New York 10016

ISBN 0-8317-0851-4

BIG CATS
was prepared and produced by
Michael Friedman Publishing Group, Inc.
15 West 26th Street
New York, New York 10010

Editor: Sharon Kalman
Art Director: Jeff Batzli
Designer: Lynne Yeamans
Layout: Charles Donahue
Photography Editor: Anne K. Price

Typeset by Bookworks Plus
Color separation by Scantrans Pte. Ltd.
Printed and bound in Singapore by Tien Wah Press Pte. Ltd.

Gallery Books are available for bulk purchase for sales promotions and premium use. For details write or telephone the Manager of Special Sales, W.H. Smith Publishers, Inc., 112 Madison Avenue, New York, New York 10016. (212) 532-6600.

Dedication

For my mother, who despite her own notable lack of interest in cats of any size or variety, has been largely responsible for my being able to travel the world in search of them.

A Word of Thanks

Anyone who studies the cats of Africa or Asia must acknowledge their debt to George Schaller of the New York Zoological Society. His field studies of these and other animals are not only thorough, but they are described in writings that show the same meticulous care. Whether a scientific report or a personal journal of his experiences, it will contain good reading as well as serious information.

There are others who have helped to make this book possible. My travels have been in the hands of a number of people over the years, but none have handled their details so deftly as Peter Celliers (representing the SATOUR in New York) and Mark Hamilton of Classic Tours International in Chicago. Each of them understood what I wanted to see and do, and each of them made sure I missed no detail.

Closer to the bush have been the rangers and guides whose first-hand information and experiences sparked my interest in the big cats. Most notable among these are Tony Williams, of Harry's Huts; Gerritt Mayer, who promised me a leopard before I left Mala Mala and kept going until we found one; and Jonathan Swart, of Inyati, who observed every detail of the bush and could explain it with infinite patience. To my hosts throughout Africa—Clive and Jane Froome of Nairobi, Susanne and Tony Blignaut of Inyati in South Africa, Phyl Palmer of Ker Downey Selby in Maun, and Barbara Jeppe of Johannesburg—goes my appreciation for their friendship and hospitality, which will remain with me even longer than the memory of my first lion. To Tim, with whom I've shared safaris from the Loldaiga Hills to Machaba, my appreciation for unfailing good humor and good company.

Nearer to home, my thanks to Sharon Kalman, an editor of extraordinary grace and good humor, and to my mother, Dee Radcliffe, for her untiring help with the research.

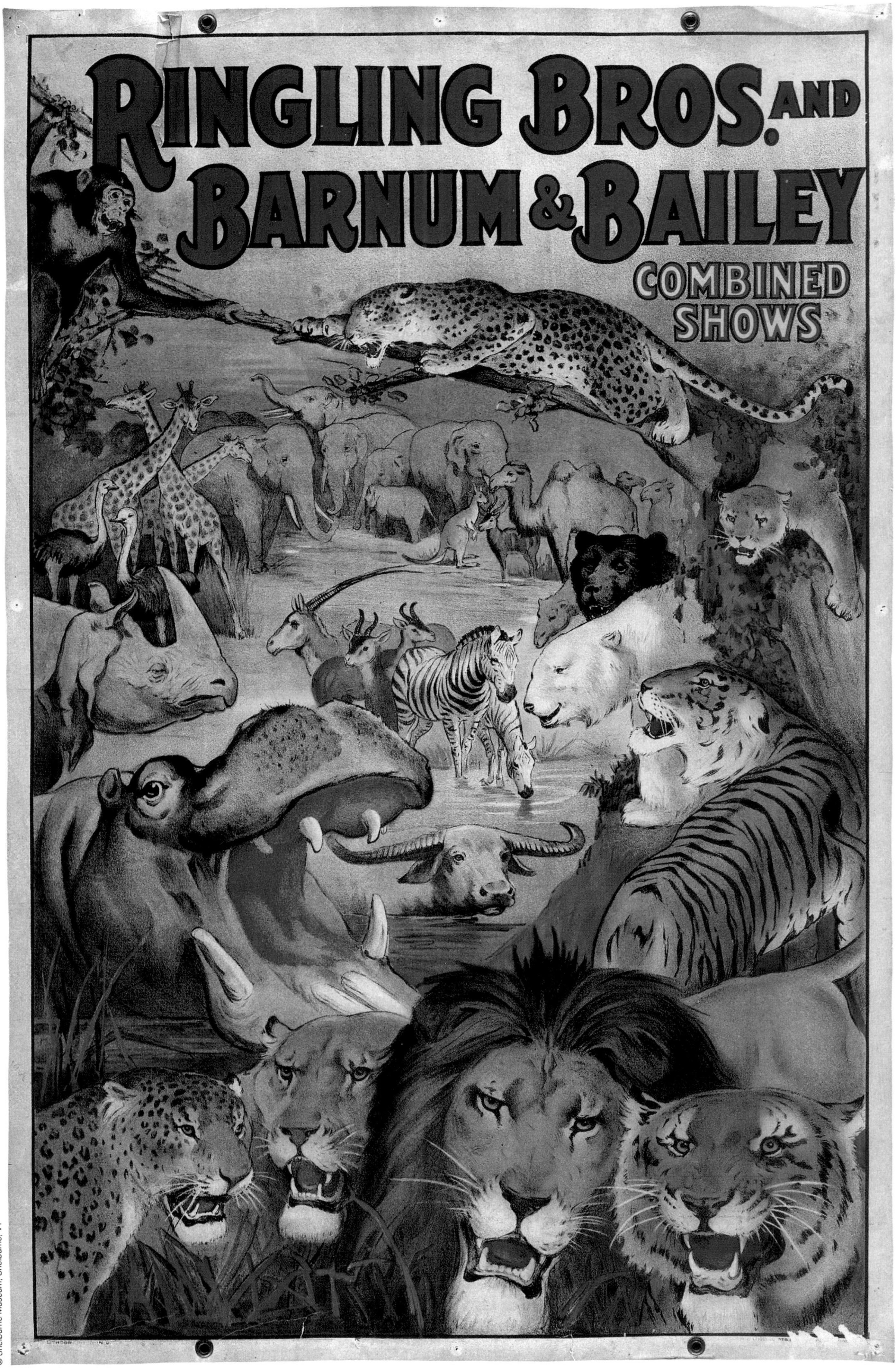
RINGLING BROS. AND
BARNUM & BAILEY
COMBINED
SHOWS

CONTENTS

Chapter One

An Introduction to the Big Cats

"A lion on the plain bears a greater likeness to ancient monumental stone lions than to the

lion which today you see in a zoo; the sight of him goes straight to the heart."

Isak Dinesen, *Shadows on the Grass*

The Myth of the Big Cats

From the prehistoric saber-toothed tiger to the highly bred Siamese, cats of all kinds have fascinated man since he first began to carve or paint impressions on the rock walls of his cave. In fact, the bigger the cat, the greater the fascination it held. As long as sixteen thousand years ago, Cro Magnons in France and Spain carved lions with considerable accuracy and artistry into surfaces of rock and bone.

The Harappan seals of the third millennium B.C. show stylized tiger portraits in a context that suggests their ritual importance in India. In texts written a thousand years before Christ, the tiger was used as a symbol of strength and power. The cheetah symbolized courage to the ancient Egyptians, who carved its likeness in friezes and other decorations. Ramses II took a lion into battle with him, Amenhotep hunted lions with bow and arrow, and the great sphinx itself has the body of a lion. Cheetahs were kept as royal pets by Charlemagne and Genghis Khan and the Cōla dynasty of India used the tiger as its symbol of power.

The lion has survived as a symbol of power into modern times; the kings of England, Denmark, and Norway have lions on their crests, as do many titled families and municipalities. It is the tiger, however, that has survived in folklore and symbolism to represent fierce fighting skills of speed and power—they are far more popular than lions as the emblems of sporting teams and military units, such as the Flying Tigers of World War II.

A militant political organization of the 1960s chose the fierce leopard as its symbol, helping to perpetuate a popular misconception of the black leopard as a separate species called panther. The leopard cults of the various African peoples consist of terrorists of a not much different sort. Jean-Pierre Hallet describes these in *Animal Kitabu*: "...humans have themselves invoked the leopard's name and aura so that they might terrorize and take human life. I refer to Africa's notorious Leopard Man secret societies, especially the Congo's still-active Anyoto which was nearly extirpated by the former colonial government and then revived by the Ituri forest tribes after the Congo received its independence."

THE MALE LION, GAZING OUT OVER THE PLAIN, IS AN IMPOSING SIGHT; HIS WHOLE DEMEANOR BESPEAKS POWER.

CATS WERE A COMMON SUBJECT OF THE EARLIEST ART FORM SURVIVING TODAY. THIS PETROGLYPH WAS FOUND IN THREE RIVERS STATE PARK, NEW MEXICO, AND DATES FROM 800 TO 1400 A.D.

© Charles Mann

In one outbreak in 1934, men of this leopard cult murdered forty-two fellow tribesmen in three months, using methods designed to simulate the attack of a leopard. Hallet describes these in grisly detail in his book, *Congo Kitabu*:

"The Anyoto masqueraded grotesquely in bark-cloth tunics and hoods marked with black spots and rings to resemble a leopard's skin. The tail of a real leopard dangled from the human leopard's rear, attached to a belt which held other important accessories: a small earthenware pot, a stick carved in the shape of a leopard's paw, and a very sharp knife. He blew into the pot to mimic the leopard's muffled snarl, he pressed the stick into the soft earth surrounding his victim's body to copy the animal's spoor [tracks] and he used the knife to sever his prey's carotid arteries. The final and most characteristic tool was an iron bracelet equipped with four dangling knives."

Hunting at dusk, the Anyoto followed the methods of the predator by avoiding strong men who would put up a fight and striking the old, children, and especially women. Often as an initiation requirement they killed their own sisters or other relatives, whom they then cannibalized.

Mary Kingsley, who explored much of West Africa in the 1890s, discussed strikingly similar societies in the Niger delta, a considerable distance from the Congo. Here they used real leopard skins as costumes, and Kingsley had the opportunity to examine one. In her book, *Travels in West Africa*, she described the claw knives in more detail:

> "Sometimes, instead of the three-pronged forks, there are fixed in the paws of the leopard skin sharp-pointed cutting knives, the skin being made into a sort of glove into which the hand of the human leopard fits. In one skin I saw down south this was most ingeniously done. The knives were shaped like the leopard's claws, curved, sharp-pointed, and with cutting edges underneath . . ."

ALONG WITH THE FIERCE, SHARKLIKE TEETH ON THE NOSE, FLYING TIGERS AIRCRAFT PORTRAYED A SMALL WINGED TIGER JUST BELOW THE COCKPIT.

© James N. Reuss

The New World's only representative of the big cats, the jaguar, has been credited with supernatural powers for thousands of years, at least since the time of the Olmecs and the Mayas. Olmec sites in Mexico show figures that are half man and half jaguar; Mayan rulers wore jaguar-skin robes and sat on jaguar thrones. Carvings show Mayan deities with physical characteristics of the jaguar.

The jaguar was believed by the Olmec and Chavin Indians to be the earthly messenger of the gods. The shaman of the Aucas, who lived deep in the Amazon rain forests, foretells the fate of his people by the prophecy of a jaguar. The symbol of the supernatural power of the shaman throughout Central and South America was (and in places, still is) a wooden seat carved in the shape of a jaguar.

ARTIFACTS DEPICTING THE JAGUAR, SUCH AS THIS BOWL FOUND IN GUATEMALA, DATING FROM 375 TO 450 A.D., ARE FOUND THROUGHOUT THE JAGUAR'S RANGE.

Photograph by Hillel Burger/Peabody Museum, Harvard University

Even today, jaguar costumes are used in ceremonies by various South and Central American peoples, and claws and teeth are still worn around the neck as amulets for protection. Similarly, lions' teeth and claws are used in parts of East Africa in the belief that they impart the invincibility of the lion to wearers. Mary Kingsley noted that leopard whiskers were a favorite of young hunters, who wore them stuck in their hair. Leopard skins offered for sale were always missing the whiskers, which had been sold separately for their magical powers.

The ability to subdue and kill big cats often was used as a test of manhood. Before the practice was recently outlawed in Kenya, a young Masai had to face a lion in battle armed only with his spear and a knife in order to enter the highest ranks of the *muran* (warrior). He had only one chance. He had to hurl the spear into the exact spot in the lion's chest that would allow it to pierce the heart, and he had to do it while the lion was springing toward him. Then he had to jump aside quickly and finish the lion off with his knife before the lion finished him. As in the Roman arena, more often than not the lion won. The elaborate shikar hunts of the maharajas and the lure of the big game hunt are perhaps both just a modified form of this Masai rite of passage.

The Ebuya Pygmies claim to be descended from the leopard, which may account for their lack of panic when they meet one in the forest. Jean-Pierre Hallet relates the story as told to him: "Long ago a leopard lay down to kitten and had a litter of talkative Pygmies instead. The father leopard accepted the situation stoically, but after a long series of Bambuti litters, he lost all patience. 'Either stop your chattering,' he told his Pygmy cubs, 'or go away from me and make your own living.' The Pygmies, who are probably the most loquacious, noisy, high-spirited people on earth, at once trooped away." And so, when an Ebuya meets a leopard in the forest, he simply stands his ground and calls out firmly for the leopard to let him pass, addressing him as "Grandfather." Evidently the leopards of the Ituri have no taste for Pygmies, since it reportedly works.

A curiously similar practice occurs among the villagers of Sumatra who call the tiger "ancestor." This seems to be more in the hope of appeasing the tiger into nonaggressive behavior by flattery rather than through an actual belief in any relationship, although the legends of western Sumatra do hold that the Agam people are descended from a tigress.

Pygmies in the forests of southern Thailand consider the tiger to be the divine avenger and assume anyone killed by a tiger must have been breaking the taboos.

In Thailand, Indonesia, Vietnam, and Malaysia, human souls are thought to transfer at death to the bodies of tigers. Jeffrey A.

Kingdom:	Animalia	All animals
Phylum:	Chordata	Endo-skeletal animals with notochords
Subphylum:	Vertebrata	Animals with back-bones
Class:	Mammalia	Those with mammary glands and body hair
Order:	Carnivora	Those which feed mainly on meat
Suborder:	Fissipedia	Those whose feet have toes for land travel
Family:	Felidae	All cats
Genus:	*Neofelis*	Having some characteristics of the genus *Panthera*, some of *Acinonyx*, and some of *Felis* (small cats)

THE CHEETAH IS THE SOLE MEMBER OF THE GENUS *ACINONYX*, WHICH DIFFERS IN SEVERAL WAYS FROM THE *PANTHERA*.

McNeely, an anthropologist and zoologist who worked for many years in Southeast Asia, and Paul Spencer Wachtel of the World Wildlife Fund, discuss this phenomenon at length in their book *The Soul of the Tiger*. They also note that living people claim to be able to become tigers at will.

"Shamans—individuals who use magical powers, especially trances, to communicate with the spirit world—often claim tigers as their closest associates and sometimes become tigers themselves. This man-tiger relationship stretches far back into prehistory. . . .

"During his trance, the shaman becomes the tiger-spirit, or weretiger—the Asian version of the European werewolf—by casting off his rational human demeanor to enter the world of magic and receive the revelations of spirits."

The Panthera and its Relatives

The earliest forms of the cat family (Felidae) branched off the evolutionary tree from the other carnivores in the late Eocene Age, about 40 million years ago.

While the big cats (genus *Panthera*) share many characteristics with the small cats (genus *Felis*), there are a few features, other than size, that distinguish them. The principal distinction being the presence of the hyoid bone at the base of the tongue in small cats. In big cats this bone is replaced by pliable cartilage, giving them the ability to roar. Small cats can purr continuously; those of the genus *Panthera* cannot.

But scientific classifications are not hard and fast; here as elsewhere there are species that fall outside the tidy definitions. The snow leopard is classed with the big cats, but does not roar and feeds in a crouched position like small cats. The cheetah, classed with the big cats, is considerably smaller than the puma, which is a *Felis*. Although classed with the *Panthera*, the cheetah is the sole member of a separate genus, the *Acinonyx*.

In old writings, the terms for all the big cats are often confusing, with "pard" and "panther" used to describe cats as diverse as the leopard, puma, or jaguar. The term panther is not a correct identification for any type of cat, although their genus is *Panthera*.

THE CLOUDED LEOPARD IS
THE SMALLEST MEMBER OF
THE FELIDAE FAMILY. IT IS
ALSO OF A DIFFERENT
GENUS, THE *NEOFELIS*.

© Zoological Society of San Diego

The clouded leopard, classed with the big cats, is smaller than the cheetah—in fact, smaller than the bobcat and caracal, both classed as small cats. The clouded leopard is a separate genus, the *Neofelis*, which has characteristics of both *Panthera* and *Acinonyx*, forming a bridge between the big cats, small cats, and the genus *Acinonyx*.

All felids have both color and binocular vision, which increases six-fold as the light source diminishes. Their eyes shine in the dark when a light is focused toward them, because a reflective layer in their eyes causes light to pass through the receptor layer twice, further increasing their night vision.

Cats' ears are shaped to catch and funnel sound waves into the inner ear; their sense of smell is good, although not as highly developed as the dog's. All have facial whiskers that act as sensors, especially useful for night hunting. Their teeth are well adapted for gripping and tearing, and their jaw is capable of a vicelike grip.

The social habits of the big cats—in fact, of all cats—vary only slightly. Except for the lion, the big cats are all solitary, although nomadic males (those without regularly established territories) may band together in small groups. Most are territorial, with certain areas that are exclusively theirs. Some have overlapping territories, sharing certain portions with others, while the lions have firm territorial boundaries that they patrol regularly to keep out any intruders.

All the big cats define their territory by scent-marking. They spray scent from anal glands onto trees, rocks, grass, or the ground at certain points in their territory, especially at its borders and in the areas they frequent the most. Other members of their species can tell from these scent messages how long ago the other animal was there, its sex, and, if female, whether it is in estrus. Along with preventing unwelcome encounters, this serves to advertise the condition of a female ready to mate.

LIKE MOST OF THE BIG CATS, THE TIGER IS A SOLITARY ANIMAL, ALTHOUGH IT MAY SHARE ITS TERRITORY WITH SEVERAL OTHERS.

"We carefully considered everything needed for at least eight months. If we forgot something, too bad—the nearest store was at Nepalganj, 160 miles south by foot. Staples such as rice and flour filled much of the 2,000 pound capacity of our chartered aircraft. Potatoes—and little else—could be bought from the nearest village, if the harvest was good.... Base camp rested on a small river two days beyond the village of Dolphu, population 200. No permanent path exists beyond the village, so we used wildlife trails and constructed log bridges where necessary to cross the Langu."

Rodney Jackson and Darla Hillard, *National Geographic*, June 1986

In general, big cats are adaptive to a variety of terrains, climates, and environments as long as they have adequate prey and cover from which to hunt. Only the lion lives in the open, although both the leopard and the cheetah will inhabit the low velds and savannahs as long as they offer the right cover. The jaguar prefers the dense rain forests, but will hunt in the grasslands if necessary.

To say that an animal is adaptive does not necessarily mean that a particular animal will change its habits in response to a changed environment. Instead, it refers to evolutionary adaptations; meaning that over many generations animals with certain genetic traits will survive as a particular environmental situation changes, whereas others will not. In this way, a genetic tendency that was present, but not utilized may become useful in subsequent generations. This process is called natural selection, wherein nature selects those that have the right characteristics for survival under whatever conditions prevail.

THE CHEETAH *(UPPER LEFT)* AND THE SNOW LEOPARD *(UPPER RIGHT)* SHOW MARKING PATTERNS DESIGNED TO CAMOUFLAGE THEM IN THEIR INDIVIDUAL HABITATS. *LEFT:* THE LION'S SOLID-COLORED, CREAMY TAN COAT BLENDS INTO THE AFRICAN SAVANNAH GRASSES.

How We Know About the Big Cats

The genus *Panthera*—which includes the tiger, lion, leopard, jaguar, and snow leopard—and the genus *Acinonyx* with its single member, the cheetah, make up the portion of the family Felidae known to us as the big cats. They are among the most difficult mammals to study, because they are, for the most part, secretive, reclusive, and nocturnal animals.

To add to the problem, most of them are increasingly rare, and often live in habitats inhospitable to man. Anyone studying the jaguar in its thick rain forests, for example, must be prepared to meet the deadly fer-de-lance snake. Snow leopard researchers must contend with foot travel over passes that even in the mildest of seasons may be blocked by sudden snowstorms.

The animals are hard to locate, and even where vehicle travel is possible, it usually requires bone-jarring miles of off-road travel. To be useful, a study has to be painstakingly thorough and carried on over a long period of time. To any but the most dedicated, living in field conditions for that long can become tedious at best.

THE SNOW LEOPARD IS PERHAPS THE MOST DIFFICULT OF THE BIG CATS TO STUDY, SINCE THERE ARE VERY FEW OF THEM AND THEIR HABITAT IS DIFFICULT TO TRAVERSE.

© Nancy Adams/Tom Stack & Associates

As a result of these and other problems, until fairly recently most studies were made on captive animals in zoos or animal parks. However, under these conditions, free of predators and with provided food, animals behave differently, thus the results of these studies often failed to produce information that was helpful in planning effective conservation strategies for animals in the wild.

As more of the big cats began to face the very real threat of extinction, with a number of their subspecies already lost, it became evident that more than random information was needed. It had to be based on a thorough knowledge of the needs and habits of each species. Within the past quarter century, detailed studies of all the big cats (including, to a more limited degree, the snow leopard) have been made in their native habitats.

These studies have been sponsored by a number of different organizations and institutions, who share not only resources and information but also the single purpose of learning how man can best protect the future of the big cats and their environments while there is still time. (For a list of these organizations, see page 118.) Often the studies and those who make them become an active voice in the protection of a species. While doing research for the New York Zoological Society's Wildlife Conservation Institute, Alan Rabinowitz became a major force in encouraging the government of Belize to convert the Cockscomb Basin into a jaguar reserve.

After a study of the snow leopard, George B. Schaller, the institute's director, was instrumental in the creation of the Shay Wildlife Reserve in Nepal, and his studies of both the Serengeti lions and the tigers of India have greatly increased the ability of wildlife managers to plan for the future of these species in the wild. In addition, Schaller's writings, detailed scientific reports of his field work and his books and magazine articles for the general public, have contributed significantly to the public's awareness of environmental issues and specific animals.

These field studies use a variety of different methods to reach their goals. Each environment is different, just as the reaction of each species is different, and the researcher must often create new methods on the spot. Rabinowitz, for example, had to design (and redesign) a cage in which to catch jaguars without injuring them, because it was impossible to fit them with radio collars by tracking them in the wild, since their habitat is nearly impenetrable.

In the course of their studies nearly all the researchers had at least one tense incident when they were reminded quickly and with frightening reality that the big cat is not only a wild animal but a very large and very fast one as well. While attaching a radio collar to a snow leopard early in his study, Rodney Jackson was bitten so seriously that he had to return to Katmandu for treatment—a trip that involved a hike of eight days just to get to the nearest airstrip.

Radio collaring is one of the ways in which the travel and territorial habits of a cat can be studied. This information is vital in planning parks and reserves. Combined with information on other species in the habitat, this tells planners how large a population an area can support and what environments they thrive in. Simply setting aside pieces of land is of no value if the land is not the right habitat.

Radio tracking requires attaching a small transmitter to the animal. This sends a signal that can be followed to find the animal—saving a lot of time when researchers need to study the animal's habits on a daily basis or record its movements for territorial studies. In difficult terrain, such as that of the jaguar or snow leopard, there is almost no other way to study the animals.

Careful field testing has led to a collar that is safe, comfortable, and secure. It allows for growth, but will not slide off or become entangled on undergrowth. The cats soon grow used to it.

Obviously, researchers cannot just walk up to a lion or jaguar in the wild and snap a collar around its neck. First, drug darts are used to anesthetize the animal, but even these have attendant problems. The animal must be close enough to assure a good hit. On feeling this, some animals may run and hide, which can be dangerous to the researcher looking for it and to the animal itself, since the drug might overtake it in an unprotected place where it is vulnerable to predators. Lions seem to be the easiest to deal with, because of their fairly nonchalant attitude toward vehicles. George Schaller found that he could approach to within twenty yards and dart the animal while it was resting or feeding without unduly disturbing it.

Jaguars, being far more timid, have to be captured in a large cage-like trap, darted, then dragged from the cage for collaring. While unconscious the animal is weighed, measured, and checked for any unusual features. The jaguar is then dragged back into the cage, and the door left loose enough so that when the jaguar is fully conscious it can get out. In Nepal, which also has difficult terrain and where researchers are limited as to what supplies they can carry, the snow leopards are caught in paw snares that hold them safely until researchers can dart them.

One problem in working with sedative drugs is finding the correct dosage. Until the researchers had worked with a few animals, they had to experiment with dosages: Too much could kill the animal, too little could endanger the researcher.

Various methods are used to take a census of a species. Valmik Thapar describes the Indian method, which involves using about 5,000 people. They choose a time when the land is at its driest and the water holes are fewer and smaller. Workers make plaster casts and trace impressions of the pug marks (tracks) around water holes and along wildlife trails and roads. Each is marked for place and time and these are analyzed by the research staff at each reserve. However, Thapar, in his book, *Tiger: Portrait of a Predator*, questions the accuracy of such methods. A single tiger, he points out, may walk several miles or more in one night, crossing into several different soils where his pug marks will appear different. It is quite possible, he concludes, to count the same tiger ten times in the same night. India's unskilled and disinterested forest service employees further increase the margin of error.

Although their studies were not carried out by scientific method, George and Joy Adamson contributed in many ways to the knowledge of lions and cheetahs. Raising orphaned cubs of each and systematically preparing them for their return to the wild gave the Adamsons more firsthand experience with these animals than many researchers had. Their observations, particularly of personality traits, are valuable in many ways.

In order to return Elsa (a lion) and Pippa (a cheetah) to their wild environment, the Adamsons had to teach them even the most subtle skills of an animal in the wild. This meant that they had to become keen observers of the habits of many animals other than the lion and the cheetah. The Adamsons also had to develop forms of communication that the animals would understand. The fact that the Adamsons were able to succeed in returning these two cats to the wild not only disproved common theories of the time, but proved that there were options for orphaned cubs other than a life in captivity.

The Adamsons were at the forefront of those who questioned whether it was enough for an animal to survive if it could not survive free. Their books and the resulting movie, *Born Free*, made the public more aware of the plight of wild animals and also stimulated interest in African wildlife conservation.

Spotlight on Research: The DeWildt Center

The cheetah has always been an enigma—secretive and shy, hard to study. Any attempts to learn more about its reproductive habits had been stymied by the fact that the cheetah hardly ever breeds in zoos. Area after area has seen its cheetah populations decline. Attempts at relocating and reestablishing cheetahs almost always have failed.

© Gerry Ellis/The Wildlife Collection

"We once attempted to re-introduce some cheetah into an area whose population seemed very low. We supplied them with radio collars and had a student follow them to record their activity. They kept moving, since they couldn't find a territory that existing cheetah hadn't already claimed. Finally they ended up in a private game park. They arrived just in time for drinks and when everyone had scattered for shelter, they settled themselves on the verandah where all the guests had been and just sat there enjoying the view."

Miriam Meltzer, interviewed at the DeWildt Center, 1987

Research was needed, but there seemed no way to carry it on successfully, since captive cheetahs did not behave like wild ones. The DeWildt Center, near Pretoria, South Africa, began its work in 1970 with a pair of cheetahs that had been given to them. The male had been captured in Namibia, where it had been raiding livestock pens. The female was a semi-tame one from the Northern Transvaal.

Working closely with the National Zoo in Pretoria, they attempted to breed the pair, but by 1974 there were still no cubs. Meanwhile they had been given several more cheetahs that had been molesting livestock. Thinking that maybe a female needed several males to choose from, they put one female together with five males, who proceeded to attack and kill her.

It was then that Dr. David Meltzer of the Victoria University Veterinary College became interested in the cheetah. He tested all the males for fertility and found most to be sterile. This was puzzling, but it was impossible to know if it was caused by their being in a group or whether this also occurred in the wild. Continuing tests showed that this condition changed from year to year.

The cheetahs were separated into different camps, each with about an acre of exclusive fenced territory. Passageways were built alongside the female camps, and males were allowed into these to promenade and stimulate the females into season. (In the wild this process is reversed, with the female announcing her condition to the male.)

After experimenting with different methods and introducing males who had been tested and known to be fertile, they finally achieved a

© Kathy Watkins/Images of Nature

© Thomas D. Mangelsen/Images of Nature

successful mating. As is now known to be true in the wild, the female's first litter was small and had a high mortality rate. But subsequent litters were raised successfully, and since then over 500 cheetahs have been born at the DeWildt Center.

Most of these cheetah litters have gone to zoos, nearly eliminating the demand, and hence the market, for poached cheetah. Although all responsible zoos agreed at CITES not to purchase rare or endangered species captured from the wild, there are still some zoos that buy from uncertain sources (or, in the case of the Tokyo Zoo, buy rare animals that they know to have been captured from the wild). The experience of the DeWildt Center has been shared with zoos, enabling several to set up successful cheetah-breeding programs of their own.

Early efforts to reintroduce cheetahs into the wild in southern Africa were not successful. The problem was not with the cheetahs; they had no trouble adjusting to freedom and were hunting within twenty-four hours of their release. But there were either other cheetahs or other lions in these parks and not enough prey for both, so the introduced cheetahs were driven out. When cheetahs were introduced into the Kruger National Park to boost a low population, the same thing happened.

OPPOSITE PAGE: **ATTEMPTS TO INTRODUCE CHEETAHS INTO AREAS WHERE THEIR POPULATION WAS SPARSE WERE RARELY SUCCESSFUL, LEADING SCIENTISTS AT THE DEWILDT CENTER TO REALIZE THAT A LOW CHEETAH POPULATION IN RELATION TO OTHER PREDATORS IS NORMAL.** *ABOVE:* **UNTIL THEY ARE OLD ENOUGH TO OUTRUN LARGER ANIMALS, CHEETAH CUBS ARE EASY PREY FOR LIONS, LEOPARDS, AND OTHER PREDATORS.**

THE NGORONGORO CRATER IN TANZANIA HAS VERY FEW TREES, SO LIONS, WHO DO NOT USE THEM FOR SHELTER, ARE THE ONLY CATS LIVING THERE.

These experiments led to important conclusions about the predator/prey balance, as well as about the number of cheetahs any given area could support. Evidently, based on the conclusions, the number of cheetahs in Kruger Park, although low, was balanced.

Learning from those early experiences, successful cheetah populations have been established in parks in Natal and the Venda, where there are no lions. Today, much of what is known about the breeding habits of the cheetah has been learned at the DeWildt Center, and that information has made it possible to protect wild populations of all big cats more successfully.

"But no matter how much we emotionally identified with our cheetahs' victims and the sadness of a fawn's end, we observed no more magnificent a sight than the spotted one, hurling itself on a victim at seventy miles an hour, every bit nature's epitome of speed and symmetry, agility and grace."

Kathrine and Karl Ammann, *Cheetah*

© Thomas D. Mangelsen/Images of Nature

The Role of Predation

The Felidae is the most carnivorous family of the entire order Carnivora. Its diet is almost exclusively vertebrates, and it is at the top of the food pyramid with almost no predators except man.

However, the role of the big cat as predator is often misunderstood. Natural human sympathies run with the frightened and seemingly helpless impala, struck down by the stealthy leopard that sneaks up on it as it nibbles grass. Because we see aggression in man rise out of anger, meanness, and vindictiveness, we equate the behavior of an attacker with the negative qualities we observe in human aggression.

CHEETAHS EAT ONLY FRESH-KILLED MEAT. WHEN THEY HAVE EATEN ALL THEY CAN, OR IF THEY ARE FOUND BY OTHER PREDATORS WHILE FEEDING, THEY WILL ABANDON THEIR KILL.

In fact, both the leopard and the impala are doing the same thing—satisfying their own hunger, building and preserving their strength to procreate, and building up a food supply for their off-spring. They are both part of the cycle called the food chain, and the fact that the impala's food is grass does not change things. The impala, like the grass it eats, is by nature a renewable resource. If, in fact, the leopard and other predators did not keep down the impala herds, there would soon be a shortage of grass and the impala would die of starvation. By preying on the impala, the leopard is not only playing its part by keeping himself fed and healthy, but he is further perpetuating the food chain by removing a predator of grass.

Beyond keeping the cycle of the food chain intact, the predator serves other purposes as well. Being opportunistic, the predator will choose the weakest and most easily killed for his prey. A buffalo or wildebeest too old to father young often leaves the herd to wander alone or take up with a tolerant herd of another species of grazer, such as zebra. These old, lone animals and others weakened by disease are the first targets of the predator. In this way, predators serve a culling function by limiting population and keeping the food supply available for the young and healthy who are still able to reproduce. As well, sick animals are removed from the herd before diseases are spread.

THE SPEED OF THE CHEETAH ENABLES IT TO BRING DOWN ANIMALS LARGER THAN ITSELF, SUCH AS THE TOPI SHOWN ABOVE.

"Such losses," George Schaller observes in his book, *Golden Shadows, Flying Hooves*, "benefit the prey rather than causing it harm. The removal of those that are physically below par helps to prevent the spread of disease, and in times of food shortage it reduces competition by leaving the available resources to those who are most likely to contribute to the well-being of the population by producing vigorous youngsters."

The predator's attack on prey is no more vicious than the grazer's attack on new shoots of green grass or the browser's attack on young leaves and new twigs of trees. While human sympathies often lie with the seemingly weaker prey, nature has provided for the whole population and the loss of a certain amount of it is presumed.

One argument often leveled against the predator is that it will consume more than it needs or can use. While this may be true of the fox in the chicken yard, it rarely occurs in the wild.

The prey, unless disabled by disease, age, hunger, or injury, is not defenseless. Prey is elusive, as well equipped to escape as its predator is to catch it. The slaughter of prey is effectively limited by its ability to avoid the predator. Because of this, the predator never knows where or when its next meal will be.

Most predators (and among the cats, the cheetah is the exception) either guard their prey and continue to eat until there is no more left,

or hide it where scavengers won't find it and return to this pantry to feed over the course of the next several days. Natural selection has favored predators with this storage trait. When a fox kills more chickens than it can eat, it is responding to this trait and taking advantage of an unusual opportunity. In the wild, this situation would rarely happen. While the predator is busy pursuing or finishing off its mark, the rest of the herd is fleeing well out of range. But when man has erected artificial barriers such as the fence around the chicken yard and the prey cannot escape or scatter, the predator will indulge in a surplus kill. It is a natural response to an unnatural situation.

There are no winners and no losers in predation. Both predator and prey are part of the perennial cycle of relationships necessary to sustain all life forms in the balance needed for the survival of each.

"Starting and looking half round, I saw the lion just in the act of springing upon me. I was upon a little height; he caught my shoulder as he sprang and we both came to the ground below together. Growling horribly close to my ear, he shook me as a terrier dog does a rat. The shock caused a sort of dreaminess, in which there was no sense of pain nor feeling of terror, though quite conscious of all that was happening. It was what patients partially under the influence of chloroform describe who see all the operation but feel not the knife. This singular condition was not the result of any mental process. The shake annihilated fear, and allowed no sense of horror in looking round at the beast."

Dr. David Livingstone, from his journal, 1853

THIS FANCIFUL ILLUSTRATION OF GLADIATOR AND LION WAS TAKEN FROM A ROMAN SCULPTURE.

Northwind Picture Archives

Cats and Man: Pet or Threat

The reputation of big cats as man-eaters is highly overblown. This is probably due to the sensational value of "beast attacks man," which the press has always found hard to resist over-publicizing in a civilized world. And in local villages where people live, work, and sleep within sight of predators who at any moment may be eyeing them for dinner, the fear of falling prey looms heavy on their conscience.

Although human meat is not high on the lion's menu, a hungry lion will eat whatever it can get. A starved or injured lion desperate for food may attack a human, as will one goaded or angered, as by the Masai in their initiation rites. Normally, a healthy lion with other prey available will not seek out humans.

But nature has its own abnormalities and probably the best known of these occurred in 1898 when a pair of male lions put a temporary stop to the construction of the Kenya-Uganda Railroad by consuming about sixty workers. After this pair was shot by Colonel J. H. Patterson, there were further similiar incidents in the area. Colonel Patterson wrote a fascinating account of the entire episode in his book *The Man-Eaters of Tsavo*. He describes the particularly daring attack of one lion, who was not killed until it had been on its bloody rampage for several months.

"A man-eating lion had taken up his quarters at a little road side station called Kimaa, and had developed an extraordinary taste for the railway staff. He was a most daring brute, quite indifferent as to whether he carried off the station master, the signalman, or the pointsman; and one night, in his efforts to obtain a meal, he actually climbed up onto the roof of the station buildings and tried to tear off the corrugated-iron sheets. At this the terrified baboo in charge of the telegraph instrument below sent the following laconic message to the Traffic Manager: 'Lion fighting with station. Send urgent succour.' Fortunately, he was not victorious with his 'fight with the station'; but he tried so hard to get in that he cut his feet badly on the iron sheeting, leaving large blood stains on the roof."

The Tsavo incident, although by far the most sensational and prolonged, is not the only one. Like the explorer and missionary David Livingstone who is quoted above, George Adamson was mauled by a lion and lived to tell the story. As game warden of a large area of northern Kenya, he was often called to investigate incidents of man-eating or livestock-eating lions. In Joy Adamson's book, *Born Free*, she made several observations from their experience with man-eaters:

"Most lions take to man-eating because they have some infirmity: either they have been wounded by an arrowhead or damaged in a trap, or their teeth are in bad condition, or they have porcupine quills in their paws, or they are very old and in this state turn to less agile forms of food than is natural to them. But there are exceptions, cases where one can only guess at the whim of nature which has induced them to hunt human flesh. Has their taste been aroused by the carelessness of the tribesmen who often sleep at night outside the thorn fence which protects their livestock? If a hungry lion who was considering the painful act of breaking through the fence to kill an animal inside were to find a dinner asleep outside, he would be tempted indeed . . . . Such a happening might well become a habit and give birth to another man-eater."

Whatever the reasons for lions acquiring a taste for human flesh, a wise man in the bush will not take foolish chances. George Adamson,

THE ATTACK ON THE EXPLORER, DAVID LIVINGSTONE, WAS CHRONICLED IN THIS CONTEMPORARY ENGRAVING, AS WELL AS IN HIS OWN JOURNALS. LIVINGSTONE WAS LUCKY ENOUGH TO SURVIVE THE ATTACK.

Northwind Picture Archives

who had no illusions about their capabilities, observed in *My Pride and Joy:* "Some fallacies about man-eaters never die and can be dangerous—for instance that only sick, wounded or elderly lions will without provocation attack people, and that it is safe to sleep out among lions. Many good men, including professional hunters, have been taken in the night, all over Africa."

Leopards, especially in Asia, have developed similar man-eating tendencies. The leopard, although timid and cautious, tends to live closer to human habitations, prowling close to and even inside villages. It has been suggested by several observers that the leopard's contact with man has largely been brought on by the animal's taste for dog meat. Leopards have been known to take extraordinary risks in their pursuit of dogs, and a number of these have resulted in human deaths. But they could not be classed as habitual man-eaters.

Most cases of leopards attacking humans in Africa have involved children, but in India there have been several incidents that have equalled the story of the man-eating lions of Tsavo. In Bhagalpur, leopards took the lives of about 350 people between 1959 and 1962.

THE LION, HOWEVER BENIGN HE MAY LOOK, IS A DANGEROUS AND OPPORTUNISTIC PREDATOR.

But an even more notorious case in Rudraprayaq involved over 125 deaths by a single leopard. For eight years, an armed populace of thousands, an army, and scores of skillful sport hunters from Europe tracked, trapped, baited, searched, and chased the leopard. When Colonel Jim Corbett finally shot it in 1926, he found it to be a very old male, its teeth broken and one foot crippled.

Of all the genus *Panthera*, jaguars are the least known to attack men. Although there are stories of the jaguar's range of attacks on humans, few are documented accounts. This is probably due to the jaguar's timidity, the impenetrable nature of its habitat, and the result-

IN INDIA, CHEETAHS WERE USED IN THE HUNT, SERVING MUCH THE SAME PURPOSE AS DOGS DO. THIS SCENE FROM A DEER HUNT WAS PHOTOGRAPHED NEAR HYDERABAD, INDIA.

Northwind Picture Archives

ing ease with which it and man can avoid encounters with each other. As Alan Rabinowitz found in Belize during his study of the jaguar, meeting one was nearly impossible even when he was trying to.

Man-eating tigers have been widely publicized in some parts of India. In the Kumaon Hills, tiger attacks were once a regular occurrence, as they were in the district of Mandla, where 200 to 300 deaths a year were once documented. But apart from these localized outbreaks and the cases of old or injured individuals turning to human prey, the tiger is naturally as timid as the jaguar.

Those who hunted them, even in the early part of the century when they were plentiful, attested to the difficulty in encountering one. Like the other big cats, the tiger avoids man whenever possible and does not ordinarily regard him as prey.

Attempts to domesticate big cats have been rare, and usually ended as the cat approached its mature size. The exception is the cheetah, which has been tamed, or at least kept as a "hunting dog" for centuries. In the days of the shikar, the great hunts of India, cheetahs were kept by the maharajas and trained to hunt bucks.

Until recent years it was not at all uncommon to see cheetahs as pets in Nairobi. In *The Spotted Sphinx*, Joy Adamson describes her first meeting with Pippa—the cheetah she raised and returned to the wild—in the dining room of the Stanley Hotel, where the cat was quite at home.

Except for the cheetah, the big cats are not well suited to domestication, and even cats born and raised in zoos retain enough of their wild instincts to be too dangerous as pets.

THE TIGER (ABOVE, LEFT) AND THE JAGUAR (ABOVE, RIGHT), ALTHOUGH DIFFERENT IN MARKINGS AND SIZE, ARE BOTH MEMBERS OF THE GENUS PANTHERA.

Chapter Two

Lion *Panthera leo*

"The ironical misfortune of the lion was that its magnificence, strength and ferocity, combined with the royal and religious mystique which has always surrounded it, made an irresistible challenge to the hunter. It was natural for the Maasai [sic] and Turkana to avenge themselves on the species that so often ravaged their herds—and for the Maasai to elevate this to a cult. It was inevitable that game wardens would take punitive action against individuals that killed cows or goats and sometimes their herdsmen. But it was unnatural and unnecessary that the hunting of lions should become quite such a fetish with white men."

George Adamson, *My Pride and Joy*

It was Aesop who first crowned the lion king of the beasts. Since that time this monarch has represented power, strength, invincibility, bravery, and grandeur—some deserved and some perhaps not. To the traveler in Africa, the sight of a lion close on, eye to eye, is etched forever in memory. Although not the rarest or most difficult of animals to spot, there is a regal bearing in the lion's indifferent stare and matter-of-fact regard of man that makes it the most impressive of experiences.

Not the swiftest nor the fiercest, not the most determined nor energetic of beasts, it is the lion's size and manner that has earned it the respect and fear of man, and of other animals. Although the lion rarely attacks, it is clearly capable of doing so at whim. If the lion is not the king, it certainly behaves and is treated like one.

Like human monarchs, the lion has lost most of its former empire. Cave paintings suggest that lions roamed far into Europe 15,000 years ago. Within the span of historic record, the lion inhabited most of Africa, India, and the Middle East, as well as Greece. The Persians encountered lions in Greece in the fifth century B.C. By the first century B.C. they had disappeared from Greece, and during the past two millennia they have vanished from the Middle East, North Africa, and the Cape of Good Hope. Outside of Central Africa, only a remnant population of fewer than 200 survives in the Gir Sanctuary. The few remaining lions of India are of the subspecies *P. l. persica*. Their manes are smaller, their coats thicker than African subspecies. Other subspecies are entirely gone. The Barbary lion, *P. l. leo*, of North Africa, and *P. l. melanochaita*, the Cape lion of South Africa, have disappeared with the encroachment of the Sahara sands and man, respectively. Early explorers and settlers of the Great Karroo described encounters with the Cape lion, but only three mounted specimens remain. The last one known to exist was killed in 1858.

In the late thirteenth century, Marco Polo described how merchants and other travelers built fires of green cane at night that burst with such a series of loud reports as it burned that it frightened the lions away. The lions were so numerous, he explained, that without the fires no one would be able to travel through the land, because it was made uninhabitable by their numbers.

Kingdom:	Animalia	All animals
Phylum:	Chordata	Endo-skeletal animals with notochords
Subphylum:	Vertebrata	Animals with back-bones
Class:	Mammalia	Those with mammary glands and body hair
Order:	Carnivora	Those which feed mainly on meat
Suborder:	Fissipedia	Those whose feet have toes for land travel
Family:	Felidae	All cats
Genus:	*Panthera*	Those cats with cartilage replacing the hyoid bone in the throat
Species:	*leo*	Lion

The Angolan lion (*P. l. bleyenberghi*) of Angola, Zaire, and Zimbabwe is endangered, as are the Sengalese lion (*P. l. senegalensis*) of West Africa and the Transvaal lion (*P. l. krugeri*). The only lion whose numbers have not dwindled below the danger mark is the Masai lion of East Africa.

The habitat of the lion is varied, but they are generally found in open savannahs, lightly wooded areas, or thirstland. In a few places, notably Lake Manyara in Tanzania and Tsavo in Kenya, lions habitually climb trees and can be found resting there. In most regions, however, the lion frequents the tall grasses, kopjes (rock outcrops), and low bushes that provide cover as it hunts.

The lion is well adapted as a predator. Like other cats it is muscular, lithe, and has short, powerful jaws. Its color may vary from a light sandy shade to rich auburn. Although rare, albino lions do exist, as do melanistic lions, almost coal black.

© Kathy Watkins/Images of Nature

© Fritz Polking/M.L. Dembinsky Jr. Photography Assoc.

SOMETIMES LIONS REST IN TREES *(ABOVE)*, BUT THEY ARE NORMALLY FOUND RELAXING ON THE GROUND *(LEFT)*.

The male is 25 to 50 percent heavier and larger than the female. It is from 8.5 to 10 ft. long and weighs up to 530 lbs. Only the male has a mane, which tends to be heavier on animals in colder climates. The mane makes the male lion more visible, and therefore not as stealthy a hunter as the female, but it also makes him look bigger. This is an advantage when two males confront each other, since the smaller animal will usually turn away without a fight, which could kill one and injure the other. In case a fight does follow a confrontation, the thick mane offers protection to the vulnerable head and neck areas.

Scientists are loath to ascribe human characteristics to animals. But George Adamson, who together with his wife, Joy, probably had more day-to-day experience with lions than anyone else in Africa, was not so hesitant. In *My Pride and Joy*, he wrote: "They are creatures of character and mood, who are not only sociable, but may be affectionate or shy, gentle or fierce, friendly or hostile, generous or possessive, mischievous or grim, impulsive or restrained, promiscuous, wanton, steady or frigid. Most are intelligent and inquisitive. The best are adventurous, loyal and brave."

YOUNGER LION CUBS ARE LEFT BEHIND DURING A HUNT, THEN BROUGHT TO THE KILL TO JOIN IN ANY LEFTOVERS.

© Tom Mangelsen/Images of Nature

The lion relies more on vision and hearing than on its sense of smell. Their voices are important in social dealings with other lions and they have a large repertoire of sounds: snorts, huffs, meows, grunts, howls, snarls, and growls, in addition to the roar. This roar, echoing off the granite boulders of the Serengeti or moving across the still brown grasses, announces to other lions that the territory is occupied. As Jean-Pierre Hallett described in *Animal Kitabu*, "When a lion roars, according to the warrior tribesmen of East Africa, he is really saying in Swahili: 'Nchi ya nani? Yangu, Yangu, YANGU!' 'Whose land is this? Mine! Mine! MINE!'"

The size of the territory occupied by a single pride varies, depending on the size of the pride and the abundance of prey. A small pride in a game-rich area might claim only eight to ten sq. mi. A pride of twenty or more in a region sparse in game might cover 150 sq. mi. A territory that large would require several males to defend it. Members of a pride do not welcome strange males to their territory.

By staying in the same area, a pride lessens the chance of encounters with outsiders. Its members also become familiar with the area and know its lookout points and hiding places as well as its prey's pattern of movement. Lions need this protected, familiar area in order to raise cubs successfully. Although nomadic lionesses do exist without pride or territory, it is more difficult for them to raise cubs.

Unlike other cats, the lion relies heavily on this cooperative community for its survival and regeneration. While it may appear that the male lion does little but sire offspring and wait for the female to bring him food, his contribution to the pride is great. Without the males to protect the boundaries, female lions would be unable to hunt as successfully or to leave the cubs in search of food.

With his larger size and greater weight, the male lion is more visible and less agile. Both of these traits work against him as a stalker of prey. On a hunt he usually walks last, following the rest of the pride. While the lion may be prompted to do this by the prospect of the first share of the meat, which he earns by being the dominant pride member (or the only share if the prey is small), he is also protecting the straggling cubs from predators. This is an adaptive behavior that works, hence lions with these traits have survived.

THE MALE LION *(TOP)* IS LARGER THAN THE FEMALE *(BOTTOM)* AND USUALLY HAS A MANE, WHICH MAKES HIM LOOK EVEN LARGER THAN HE ACTUALLY IS.

The males in a pride may change. A younger lion replaces an older one, normally after a battle. Rarely do these rivals fight to the death, for a lion's instinct for survival is too great. Realizing himself bested, the loser usually will leave willingly. If the challenger is no match for the resident male, he will often realize this as soon as he sees its full size and hears the resonance of the roar, and leave without a scratch. There are usually two or three adult females to each adult male in the pride, and the number of offspring is about equal to the number of adults. About half will be cubs and the other half subadults, not yet ready to leave the pride.

Prides break down into smaller groups of three to six and may remain separated but still part of the same pride. The size of these subgroups may depend on the size of the available prey. Lions whose primary food is zebra can live in larger groups with enough to share at a kill, whereas those that must live on smaller game will have fewer in a subgroup.

A pride is a companionable group. Lions of the same sex will greet each other by licking faces, rubbing cheeks, or touching noses. They often sleep with their bodies touching. While male lions tend to restrict physical contact with females to mating, they do play with cubs, or at least they tolerate a lot of ear nibbling and tail chasing. Cubs and subadults play and tussle endlessly among themselves.

There are several likely reasons why natural selection would work in favor of the social lion to create this system of prides. In the open terrain inhabited by lions, cooperative hunting is far more successful than solitary hunting. This is borne out by the observations of several researchers that prides in denser areas where hunting is hard tend to be smaller. Several lions together can surround the quarry. A group is much better able to take down a larger animal, such as a buffalo, which a single hunter could not do.

In a pride, one member can be spared to watch over all the cubs, or bring them to a kill. Injured lions, those about to give birth, or cubs whose mothers die can survive more easily in a group where the food is shared.

George Schaller, who spent three years studying lions in the Serengeti, grew able to recognize individual lions and follow the events in their lives over a long period of time. He writes in *Golden Shadows, Flying Hooves* of a particular lion: "A young female of the Masai pride was bitten in the thigh during a scuffle. A canine must have injured a nerve, for her leg withered up until she could barely hobble. Completely unable to hunt, she subsisted entirely on the kills made by others of the pride for nearly nine months before recovering the use of her leg."

The lion will exert itself as little as possible in the search for food, and spends at least twenty out of every twenty-four hours resting. They walk in search of prey or to mark a territory, usually at a very

© Kathy Watkins/Images of Nature

LIONS ARE THE ONLY BIG CATS THAT LIVE A COMMUNAL LIFE, SHARING THE RESPONSIBILITIES OF HUNTING AND CARING FOR THE YOUNG.

slow gait. In a single day they may travel as little as a mile or two, or as much as ten. In the midst of an excursion of any length, lions are likely to drop to the ground and rest without regard to the visibility of the spot. They are without predators and have no fear of resting in plain sight of any beast of the savannah or forest.

The lion is an opportunistic feeder; it will eat whatever comes along. This includes birds, fish, rodents, reptiles, and other small animals. But the main source of food is mammals weighing 100 lbs. or more. Hunting may take place at any time, especially if there is good cover, but in open areas the lion is more likely to hunt at night or in the early evening and dawn hours.

THE FEMALE LION STALKS ITS PREY *(ABOVE)* **SLOWLY AND SILENTLY, UNTIL SHE IS CLOSE ENOUGH FOR THE FINAL SHORT CHASE** *(BELOW)*.

The females, usually in pairs or small groups, lead the hunt, often with the subadults following. If the cubs are able to travel the distance, they may come next, with the males following. Lions rely on intelligence as well as strength when stalking prey.

Because they do not run as fast as many of the animals they chase, the lion must stalk as close as possible. She hides low in the underbrush or grass, advancing slowly and silently, waiting until the prey is inattentive for an instant. Then she makes the final dash, knocking

the prey to the ground with her powerful paw. Groups hunting together will fan out into a crescent, making escape more difficult. Sometimes they will completely encircle a small herd, each downing one as the prey scatters.

Small game is usually slapped down with a blow of the paw, then bitten through the neck. Larger prey is killed by a grip on the throat that brings on eventual suffocation. The lion usually eats the meat on the spot.

FEMALE LIONS WAIT (ABOVE) UNTIL THE MALE LION HAS EATEN BEFORE SHARING THE REMAINDER OF THE KILL (BELOW).

Whenever it can, the lion will save its energy by letting another animal do the stalking and chasing. While seemingly at rest during the heat of the day, the lion will scan the sky for signs of vultures circling or hovering over a kill in progress. Following the vultures to the spot, the lions will drive away the hyenas who made the kill. One or two lions are able to drive off a pack of ten or more hyena.

The male lion eats first, until he is full. He is followed by the females. Cubs come last, with the strongest and scrappiest getting most of the meat. By the time the male has eaten, and then the females, there is often little left for hungry cubs. Cubs under five months rarely accompany the hunt unless the kill is a large animal. If the cubs have not accompanied the hunt, the mother eats before going back for them. The male lion, after eating, may save a portion for the cubs by not allowing the females to eat it first. The result is that unless food is very scarce, cubs rarely starve. They do learn to be fast and aggressive in their battle for food, however, a valuable trait if they are to survive.

While by their size and agility females are better designed for hunting than males, nomadic males without anyone to hunt for them are quite capable of providing food for themselves. They have to work a little harder, with a higher percentage of unsuccessful chases, but they are still good hunters.

Zebra, wildebeest, gazelle, buffalo, and warthog, along with reedbuck and other antelope, make up the bulk of the lion's diet. George Schaller, during his research in the Serengeti, ascertained that a female lion requires 6,000 lbs. of prey a year, and a male 8,400 lbs. He converts that to about ten zebra per year for a female.

Lions in the wild are ready to mate at the age of three or four years, with females coming into estrus more than once a year. A female lion, without cubs, comes into heat about every three weeks. During this time both males and females may be active for a period of several days, mating often. This frequency is necessary since it is the act of repeated mating that causes the lioness to ovulate.

Gestation is between 100 and 119 days, short for an animal of this size. Litters may vary from one to five, but are usually of two or three cubs weighing 3 lbs. each. It is three weeks before cubs can walk. At five to seven weeks they are old enough to join the pride, at which time they may be nursed by other females or watched by other pride members when their mother is hunting. They are frequently left alone in tall grass or brush.

AS IS TRUE WITH OTHER CATS, THE LION IS ATTENTIVE AND PROTECTIVE OF ITS YOUNG.

During the dry season, when there is little or no grass to attract grazers, cub mortality is often high. But this is a normal response to a shortage of food and keeps the numbers in line with the food supply by eliminating the weakest members, instead of endangering the entire population.

Although cubs over five months old may, and often do, watch the hunt, they do not take part until they are at least a year old. By the time they are two years old they are full members of the pride, hunting and sharing more fully in the kill. They may still lack the skill of

© Tom Mangelsen/Images of Nature

LION CUBS LEARN COORDINATION AND QUICK RESPONSES FROM THEIR TUSSLING AND PLAYING (ABOVE). YOUNG LIONS (OPPOSITE PAGE) REMAIN WITH THE PRIDE UNTIL THEY ARE TWO OR THREE YEARS OLD.

older lions, but continue to learn by participating. Although it is frequently stated that the tussling and playing of cubs is actually training for the hunt, experts doubt this. The two activities have little in common except to encourage the development of coordination and fast movement.

From the ages of two-and-a-half to three-and-a-half, males leave the pride. Some females also leave at that age and become nomadic, although it is not exactly understood why this happens. These nomadic animals are difficult to study since they generally leave the area or live at its edge for a time before disappearing entirely. The young males leave as a group and may, still as a group, take over an existing pride as the dominant males. It is not unusual for newly

arrived males to kill the cubs of the previous males. This behavior assures that a greater number of the new males' genes will be passed on to new offspring, since a female without cubs comes into estrus quite soon.

The process of young males leaving the pride and taking over another as a group is known as outbreeding. It assures a changing genetic structure and prevents inbreeding.

Although hunting was responsible for the depletion or extermination of lions in Europe, India, and elsewhere, it is the encroachment of man into the lion's habitat that is the most serious threat today. Hunting has been outlawed or strictly controlled in most countries. But the increasing demands of exploding African populations continue to push in on the wildlands that are the lion's home.

Lions require space because the grazing populations that are their food supply need vast areas to feed in and migrate through. As more land goes to agriculture there is ultimately less space for the lions.

A FEMALE LION GUARDS A KILL FOR THE MALE, WAITING TO EAT UNTIL THE MALE HAS TAKEN HIS SHARE.

© Gerry Ellis/The Wildlife Collection

Also, as crop and livestock grazing areas move closer to the boundaries of parks and protected areas, predators such as lions wander into those areas and molest (or are blamed for molesting) cattle, sheep, and goats, and are shot by farmers. This was the fate of the Cape lion before reserves and parks were created to protect them.

In some places, man-made changes in habitat have created overpopulations of lions. Etosha National Park in Namibia, one of the world's largest with 8,400 sq. mi. supports 500 lions. This is thought to be the most dense in Africa. In 1973 the park was fenced to protect its wildlife from neighboring tribesmen and farmers. That cut off natural migration routes and put serious pressure on the remaining grazing land. The springbok were able to survive on the encroaching bush and new grasses, but zebra and wildebeest herds began to weaken and decline. Lions found it even easier to eat, with their prey more dependent upon the grasses near the water holes. Lions drove off the cheetahs that had previously preyed on the springbok, and their numbers rose. The park was obviously out of balance.

WITHOUT INTERFERENCE BY MAN, WILD POPULATIONS OF PREY AND PREDATOR WILL USUALLY STAY BALANCED IN ANY PARTICULAR AREA.

One option was to cull lions and springbok, but nature has a way of compensating for culled lions, as researchers had discovered in Kruger Park. There, more cubs survived and kept up the pride's numbers.

Instead, biologists injected slow-release birth-control pills into female lions in an attempt to control the runaway population until the balance reestablished itself.

In the Eastern Transvaal, the loss of lion habitat to agriculture was halted by the establishment of Kruger National Park and the adjacent private game reserves of the Sabie Sand. Although the Kruger Park's lion's numbers aren't great, they are stable and are in line with the available land area (roughly the size of the state of Massachusetts) that they occupy. The Zimbabwe and Botswana lion populations are stable. Although the lion is not considered an endangered species, it is listed as threatened worldwide due to its diminishing habitat in eastern Africa.

The best places to actually see lions in the wild are in the Masai Mara in Kenya, the Serengeti and the Ngorongoro Crater in Tanzania, the central plains of Kruger National Park, and the Sabie Sand reserves in the Eastern Transvaal. There is also a very good chance of seeing lions at Samburu, Amboseli, and Tsavo in Kenya, Lake Manyara (where lions rest in the trees) in Tanzania, Shindi Island in the Okavango Delta, and Mashatu in the Tuli reserves, both within Botswana.

Although you are likely to see lions during the daytime in any of these places, the best time to follow them on a hunt is in the evening or on a night drive, especially where off-road travel is permitted. This is usually possible only in private reserves. The combination is by far the best lion-watching experience, especially when coupled with daytime drives for easier photography. Night drives are standard at Inyati, Mala Mala, Kirkman's, and Harry's Huts in the Sabie Sand, and at Mashatu and Shindi Island in Botswana. They are possible in the Ngorongoro Crater only if you travel with an outfitter who is licensed to camp in the crater. Only those camped on the crater floor can stay or travel there after sunset. (See page 114 for information on safaris.)

THE TEETH OF A LION ARE DESIGNED FOR TEARING MEAT.

Chapter Three

Tiger *Panthera tigris*

"The natural history of the tiger has been studied predominantly along the sights of a rifle..."

George B. Schaller, *The Deer and the Tiger*

prey. The tiger can, however, adapt to a wide variety of forests, from mangrove swamps and rain forests to high altitude coniferous forests—even to tall grasslands.

The primary reason that the tiger needs good cover is that it is built for stalking its prey, not chasing it on the run. Its body is long, bulky, and heavy in the shoulders, with a small head and short, powerful legs. The male of each species is heavier and longer than the female. Indian tiger males are about 6 ft. long, and females 5 to 5.5 ft. The male may weigh between 350 and 600 lbs., with females averaging about 300 lbs.

© Gerry Ellis/The Wildlife Collection

THE DARK STRIPES OF THE TIGER BLEND INTO THE SPECKLED PATTERNS OF SUNLIGHT AND SHADE IN THE FORESTS WHERE IT LIVES.

The tiger's black stripes vary in width and pattern and lie on a coat ranging in color from cream to orange to rust. The underside of all tigers is a cream color.

There have been few studies of the tiger in the wild. In 1963, George Schaller, then a research associate at Johns Hopkins University, spent over a year observing tigers and their prey in the Kanha National Park in central India. In 1976 Valmik Thapar conducted field studies of tigers at another reserve, Ranthambhor, somewhat north of Kanha. Most of what is known about tigers in the wild is based on studies of the Indian tiger.

The work of these researchers has brought a new picture of the habits of the tiger. Previously considered a solitary animal because they had rarely been observed in groups, the tiger has been found to meet casually without confrontation and at times will share a kill. While they do not live in prides as lions do, they may share their territory with others with whom they may be sociable.

Territories for any one tiger were found to be about twenty-five sq. mi., but these vary from place to place depending on the supply of prey. Along with the regular residents of an area, whose territories may either be exclusive or overlap extensively, there may be nomadic males. There is usually one dominant male in an area, but he may tolerate transient males. Females seem to share their domain easily with both males and other females.

Although the closed nature of the tiger's habitat and the size of the game usually make solitary hunting the most efficient, tigers have been observed in group hunts, behaving much as lions do. When the kill is a large one, even if it was taken by a solitary hunter, it is not unusual for it to be shared by other adults as well as the cubs.

Like other large predators, the tiger spends much of its time conserving energy for the hunt. As much as 80 percent of its day may be spent resting or sleeping. Early morning and late evening are often spent grooming, with the tiger licking its fur, much like a house cat.

The tiger usually hunts at night, hidden from its prey by vegetation and darkness. It may walk for miles in search of food, whenever possible along streambeds, paths, and roads.

THE TIGER STALKS ITS PREY TO WITHIN CLOSE RANGE BEFORE A FINAL LUNGE BRINGS IT DOWN. TIGERS ARE NOT GOOD RUNNERS.

When prey is spotted—and this is thought to be by sight and sound rather than smell—the tiger creeps closer under cover of grasses, trees, or bushes. Moving very carefully, with slow and silent steps and usually in a crouch, the tiger moves to within sixty ft. or less for the final rush. This spring allows the tiger to cover the distance in a few bounds, with a tremendous momentum that may knock the prey to the ground. If the prey has started to run, the tiger may slap at its legs with a forepaw to knock it down.

Even when the prey is heavier than the tiger, a bite to the throat usually suffocates it. To avoid vultures, the tiger normally drags the dead animal into the bushes or under trees. If the prey is very large, the tiger will stay with it for several days, eating frequently.

The tiger's method of attack varies with the prey and the situation, and a wide variety of methods have been recorded. For all the tiger's strength and speed, observers agree that only about one attack in twenty results in a meal.

Just as the tiger is versatile in its method, it is catholic in its taste for food. The various deers—the chital, sambar, nilgai, and others—make up the tiger's main diet, with wild pig, birds, the langur monkey, even frogs and lizards filling in when available. The tiger will attack and kill livestock when there is not enough wild prey, or if it is easier to get.

Although observers since the early moguls agree that the tiger is a nocturnal hunter, Valmik Thapar observed some interesting deviations during the 1980s. First he noticed that tiger sightings had increased nearly tenfold since he began studying them four years earlier. Tiger tracks were found on traveled roads and there were sightings of tigers in open areas. The tigers seemed more active and more casual about being seen.

Then Thapar began to see tigers hunting in the daytime. These were not isolated cases of animals whose hunger had driven them to extraordinary behavior. While the increased sightings could be explained by the increase in the park's population from fourteen to forty tigers, this did not explain the relaxed attitude of the tigers toward being seen and hunting in broad daylight. After observing these phenomena, Thapar developed an interesting theory.

© Gerry Ellis/The Wildlife Collection

THE TIGER HAS A WIDE RANGE OF PREY, EATING ANYTHING FROM BIRDS TO FROGS WHEN LARGER GAME IS SCARCE.

Not long before he arrived at the Ranthambhor reserve in the late 1970s, the first protective restrictions prohibited hunting of any of the wild animals. For centuries the tiger had been hunted and each generation had taught the next to stay under cover and out of sight. But the villages within the reserve had been moved and the sound of firearms was no longer heard.

Thapar advances his theory in his book *Tiger: Portrait of a Predator:*

"But from 1979 onwards there was no human encroachment. New generations of tigers were being born to mothers who had never known man's aggression. The mother was no longer teaching them to avoid man since there was none [sic] to avoid except for the occasional Jeep-load of curious observers. The tigers were once again coming into their own. They were using both night and day to hunt and were following the seasonal movements and behavior of the deer and antelope. It was no longer necessary for them to stick to the dense areas of the forest; they were quite confident walking on roads, open grasslands and even around Jogi Mahal. The tigers' whole perception had changed—they were now the fearless kings of the jungle and man, the respectful observer, had been removed from his dastardly role as a predator. But it had taken ten years of complete protection in Ranthambhor for the fear to be removed."

The tiger does not appear to have clear-cut mating seasons, and cubs are born at any time of year. Litter size varies from one to seven, and cubs are hidden in a cave or under the protection of overhanging rocks or in a hollow tree. The mother leaves them alone while she hunts, and after six or eight weeks they begin to eat the food she brings them. As soon as they can move about, the cubs follow on hunts, where they remain silent and hidden.

Unlike the lion, which eats before allowing the cubs a share, the tiger brings the meat to the cubs and they all share in the spoils. When the female shares a kill with others, the male "guest," instead of eating first, waits for the mother and cubs to eat before beginning.

The mortality rate within the first few months of the cubs' birth reaches 50 percent, and the female tiger is very aggressive in protect-

© Northwind Picture Archives

IN ADDITION TO TIGERS TAKEN BY HUNTING PARTIES OF THE RAJ, INDIAN MAHARAJAHS FELLED TIGERS LITERALLY BY THE THOUSANDS.

ing them. Cubs are very playful, wrestling and stalking each other. As they grow stronger, at about six months, they begin to learn hunting skills. The mother not only must protect the cubs from predators and teach them to hunt, but they hunt for food as well. As they grow, so does their appetite, and this is a busy time for the mother. When they have learned some of the basic hunting skills, the mother may bring the cubs an injured, but mobile, animal to practice hunting.

As the cubs become more skillful, the mother will leave them alone for longer and longer periods to hunt on their own. She checks on them frequently to be sure they are catching enough food. At about twenty months the cubs begin to live on their own. Although the father is not part of the family group, fathers have been observed returning briefly and playing with the cubs.

The most rapid decline of the tiger population, particularly in India, has been since the middle of the nineteenth century. Hunting records show one or two kills a day, indicating an enormous tiger population. The Maharaja of Udaipur shot over 1,000 in his lifetime, and in 1965 another maharaja claimed to have shot over 1,100.

In addition to sport hunting, there was a deliberate destruction of tigers by farmers who feared attacks on livestock. In some places there was a bounty on them. As agricultural poisons became available, farmers left out buffalo carcasses laden with insecticides.

While the tiger was being hunted down in a concerted attempt to exterminate it, its forest homes were being cut down and plowed up for crops and homes. Villages sprang up where the tiger had once hunted for deer. As the human population of India increased at phenomenal rates, the tiger population fell from 40,000 in 1900 to 4,000 in 1960. By 1972 it had dropped to under 2,000. The hunting stopped (at least officially) in 1972, as did the sale of tiger skins. But encroachment on the places where tigers lived continued unabated, and villagers continued to kill them illegally.

The International Union for the Conservation of Nature (IUCN) and the World Wildlife Fund joined with conservationists in India to begin Project Tiger, and in 1973 nine areas were set aside as reserves. Six more, some of them in neighboring countries, have been added since then. Entire villages were relocated out of these areas, and although logging and other commercial activities still continue in

LOCAL VILLAGERS TRAPPED TIGERS IN LARGE NETS, AS IS SHOWN IN THIS ENGRAVING OF A SCENE NEAR MYSORE.

some of them, they are at least providing a safer haven for the tiger. Populations have stabilized and begun to increase in these reserves.

All subspecies of tiger are listed as endangered, and will probably continue to be because of the isolated nature of the areas where they are found. These pockets can support only so many predators and there is no way to connect them for better genetic mix. India's human population continues to increase and its forests continue to decrease, leaving tigers outside the reserves in a rapidly diminishing habitat.

Only about 1,500 tigers live in the reserves, and the future of the rest is uncertain at best. And even those in the reserves are not entirely safe. At Ranthambhor, one of the smallest and easiest to guard, there have been a number of alarming incidents. Although villages had been moved from the reserve, surrounding farmers made constant forays into the park to cut fodder and bring in cattle for grazing. Under this kind of pressure it is difficult to guard even the 154.5 sq. mi. of that park. Larger parks are impossible.

Aggressive farmers and livestock, traveling on foot and cutting vegetation, have disturbed the wildlife and disrupted their normal patterns, so hunting becomes more difficult for the tiger. Thapar witnessed groups of grass cutters in the park confronting a tiger, and the park guards have been stoned, even killed, when they tried to stop farmers from grazing their herds in the park. With one billion head of livestock grazing in India, and its population still increasing, Project Tiger has a great deal of work cut out for it. Education in the rural areas would seem to be an important priority if the tiger is to survive.

Southern Thailand's largest remaining lowland forest is being protected as part of the existing wildlife sanctuary at Khao Ang Ru Nai. Residents of the six villages there have been relocated, and, with the help of the Thai army, illegal logging has been curtailed.

Not all of India's tiger reserves have facilities for visitors. Ranthambhor was once a massive royal fortress, one of India's oldest. The ruins sit atop a cliff, looking out over a broad valley with lakes and forests, all of which was once the hunting estate of the Maharaja of Jaipur. It is one of the most beautiful settings for tiger-watching, since the animals can sometimes be found in the ruins of the palace or under the enormous banyans that form an architecture all their own.

The Sariska Reserve is also set in dry deciduous forests edged by cliffs. Its open grass-covered areas are inhabited by large herds of nil-gai, an ungainly antelope also known as the blue bull.

Possibly the best known of the tiger reserves is Nepal's Royal Chitwan National Park, where game-viewing is done from the backs of elephants. From this vantage point, visitors can easily see over the tall grasses and travel over terrain that a wheeled vehicle would not be able to cover. The elephant can also approach game more closely, giving a better chance of unobstructed views.

© Gary Randall/FPG International

OPPOSITE PAGE: THE SIBERIAN TIGER IS DIFFICULT TO SEE IN THE WILD, ALTHOUGH THERE ARE SAFARIS INTO ITS PRESERVES. THE WHITE BENGAL TIGER *(LEFT)* IS RARELY SEEN, ALTHOUGH IT HAS BEEN SIGHTED AT BANDHAVGARH NATIONAL PARK.

The Bandhavgarh National Park in central India lies within one of India's few remaining areas of natural forest. It is an area of meadows and grassland, with bamboo clumps and a semi-deciduous forest with an undulating terrain of hills and valleys. Although a small park, and with only one camp for travelers, it is known as the best park for daylight viewing of tigers. Rare white tigers have been seen here, as well as some of the few remaining leopards in Asia.

While there are reserves set aside for the protection of the Siberian tiger, they have been difficult to get to and the chances of seeing the tiger in the dense forests are remote. There are, however, special safaris into these areas of Manchuria and Siberia, led by expert guides and trackers, which increases the chance of seeing these tigers in their wild habitat. (See travel sources, p. 114).

Chapter Four

Leopard *Panthera pardus*

"For my part, I found the leopards much more alarming than the lions. They seemed to me to be the most beautiful of all the animals, the most lithe and wild.... There is a hair-trigger ferocity about the leopards. Each time one lifted one's binoculars for a closer view one was confronted with two green glaring lamps that burned directly into one's own eyes. The pupils had the effect of boring into you. No animal, not even the lion, has such an implacable gaze."

Alan Moorehead, *No Room in the Ark*

"The real king of beasts," states Jean-Pierre Hallet in *Animal Kitabu*, "is the leopard." Not as thoroughly studied as the lion, man's fascination with the leopard may spring from its elusive habits, its air of mystery, and its aura of danger.

The most adaptable and hence widely distributed of all the big cats, the leopard has learned to live near man. Despite the justified fear it inspires in man and despite the value of its spotted hide, the leopard has survived. Its wits and skills as a hunter and fugitive, even its attractive coat, make it elusive and hard to find.

Rudyard Kipling, in *The Jungle Book*, speaks of the leopard's ability to make itself invisible, as it was believed to do by many in India. It is easy to see the origins of this folk belief when trying to distinguish a leopard from the dappled pattern of sunlight that filters through the leaves of an acacia tree. In the dense forests of India, seeing a leopard only a few feet away is nearly impossible.

The leopard is not well suited to confinement. Lions and cheetahs can be raised as pets, but a baby leopard, however engaging as a kitten, soon becomes vicious. The director of a European zoo once questioned why any zoo would want a leopard, when a cheetah or lion can be kept safely. Yet of all the big cats, it is the leopard that breeds prolifically in captivity, another sign of its immense adaptability.

The leopard is found throughout sub-Saharan Africa and southern Asia, with scattered populations in China and North Africa. Its habitat requirements are few: some cover and a supply of prey. Temperature, terrain, flora, and other predators are of little concern, since the leopard lives well in the savannahs, rain forests, mountain elevations, and even quite close to cities.

Subspecies include the Amur leopard (*P. p. orientalis*), now endangered but still surviving in parts of North China and Korea, where its thick coat of longer hair protects it from severe winters. The Anatolian leopard (*P. p. tulliana*) of Asia Minor, the Barbary leopard (*P. p. panthera*) of Morocco, Algeria, and Tunisia, the Sinai leopard (*P. p. jarvisi*) of the Sinai desert, and the South Arabian leopard (*P. p. nimr*) are all endangered as well. Each of these survives as a small or isolated population. The Zanzibar leopard (*P. p. adersi*), whose spots are very small, is believed to be extinct.

THE FAVORITE DAYTIME RESTING PLACE OF THE LEOPARD IS IN AN ACACIA TREE HIGH ABOVE THE PLAIN.

Kingdom:	Animalia	All animals
Phylum:	Chordata	Endo-skeletal animals with notochords
Subphylum:	Vertebrata	Animals with back-bones
Class:	Mammalia	Those with mammary glands and body hair
Order:	Carnivora	Those which feed mainly on meat
Suborder:	Fissipedia	Those whose feet have toes for land travel
Family:	Felidae	All cats
Genus:	*Panthera*	Those cats with carti-lage replacing the hyoid bone in the throat
Species:	*pardus*	Leopard

Only the North African leopard (*P. p. pardus*) is not considered endangered, although it is a threatened species because of the value of its fur on the black market. It is found throughout sub-Saharan Africa and South Asia.

The so-called black panther is no more than a melanistic leopard, in which a recessive gene has caused it to have a black coat. Under a direct light the spot patterns of this leopard are visible, but until a century ago its status as a separate species was still argued.

The recessive gene causing the black coat is far more common in Asia and in forest and mountain areas than in Africa. In the Malay peninsula nearly half of the population is said to be black.

Black leopards are more aggressive than spotted ones, although the two types may be born in the same litter. Ludwig Koch-Isenburg reports a possible explanation in *The Realm of the Green Buddha*, although he does not find it entirely satisfactory:

"Everyone who travels in tropical regions knows what perfect camouflage a spotted coat provides. Spotted arboreal creatures literally disappear in the play of lights and shadows created by the foliage of a tree. I myself once stood for some time under a mighty giraffe acacia in East Africa, watching some antelopes grazing on the plain, and my native guide had to call my attention to a leopard stretched out on a branch above, staring fixedly at us. Even at that, it took several moments before my eyes could pick the animal out of its surroundings. It is argued, then, that a predator who lacks this camouflage is at a disadvantage in hunting creatures like monkeys, which depend on their eyesight for protection. Since the black panther has the wrong coloring—"wrong" in the biological sense—he must make up for this in being more ferocious in attack, must leap sooner, and must be more tenacious in pursuit."

If less is known about the leopard than about the lion, it is because the leopard is so difficult to study. Although it can survive closer to inhabited areas than other big cats, it succeeds by being very cagey by making itself "invisible." Scientists trying to study the leopard are severely hampered by this. Unlike the lion, the leopard clings to the cover of trees, kopjes, dense vegetation, and low scrub and thickets.

© Gerry Ellis/The Wildlife Collection

TODAY, THE BLACK LEOPARD IS RARELY FOUND ON THE AFRICAN CONTINENT, BUT IN SOME PARTS OF ASIA IT OUTNUMBERS THE MORE COMMON SPOTTED VARIETY.

In the Serengeti, leopards are most often seen in the large acacia trees, where they lie with their tail and often a leg or two draped over a branch. Although they are most visible there, they are safe, for their only predator is the lion, which will not climb a tree after one.

Male leopards are thought to have definite territories, while female leopards' territories overlap with those of males and other females. They are solitary, avoiding both meeting and confrontation with other leopards, although they live in the same territory for many years.

OPPOSITE PAGE: **THE BEST WAY TO FIND A LEOPARD IN THE SERENGETI IS TO LOOK FOR THE SPOTTED LEGS AND TAIL DRAPED OVER A LIMB.** *BELOW:* **THE LEOPARD, UNLIKE THE LION, DOES NOT ROAR.**

© Kathy Watkins/Images of Nature

The leopard is capable of making a variety of sounds, but is not very vocal. It has a rasping, coughlike call and may also snarl, hiss, and growl when angry or alarmed.

Leopards hunt alone, stalking stealthily until they are close enough to attack in a short sprint. They hunt at night, and much of their quarry is small—the genet, civet, monkey, birds (including ostrich), fish, reptiles, bush pig, and jackal. Although a full-grown wildebeest

THE LEOPARD SPENDS A
GREAT PART OF ITS DAY IN
THE TREES. FROM HERE IT
CAN SPOT PREY, AND IT IS IN
THE TREES THAT IT HIDES
ITS KILL.

is hard for a solitary leopard to kill, one occasionally succeeds. Immature wildebeest are more common, along with the full range of grazers—gazelle, impala, small hartebeest, klipspringer, steenbok, duiker, reedbuck, and various others. They are known to take animals up to 250 lbs., but are more likely to attack the foals of animals such as zebra and topi.

The leopard usually hides its kill, often dragging it up a tree to hang over a branch. Here it is safe from piracy by a lion and will keep for several days for continued feeding. If left on the ground, the meat would have to be guarded continuously from hyenas, lions, vultures, and others. Although lions could climb trees to reach the meat, they don't seem to notice it above their line of scent and vision. Nor do vultures normally scavenge the leopard's kill, although reaching it would be no problem. It has been suggested that this is because vultures depend on their keen eyesight to spot a kill, and prey wedged in the fork of a tree is covered from above by foliage.

Leopards are particularly fond of dogs as food, and whenever they are near habitations where dogs are kept they take advantage of the opportunity—even though it is at great risk to the usually cautious leopard. They will prowl in villages and houses for even a small dog.

Throughout Africa and India, the local peoples have legends to explain such unusual behavior. Jean-Pierre Hallet, who has collected folktales in Africa, relates the explanation from the eastern Ituri in his book *Animal Kitabu*: "The leopard once planted a field of peanuts which was then raided by a lizard. To escape punishment, the lizard told the leopard that he had seen a dog digging in the field. Enraged, Chui [the leopard] went to search through all the forest for the thief who stole his peanuts. 'To this very day,' I was told, 'he is still trying to find the right dog.' "

Mary Kingsley records another explanation from that part of the continent in *Travels in West Africa*: "Leopards always come after dogs, because once upon a time the leopard and the dog were great friends, and the leopard went out one day and left her whelps in charge of the dog, and the dog went out flirting, and a snake came and killed the whelps, so there is ill feeling to this day between the two."

THE ADULT LEOPARD HAS NO PREDATORS; OCCASIONALLY, A LION WILL SNATCH AN UNPROTECTED CUB, BUT OTHER ANIMALS KEEP THEIR DISTANCE.

Leopards have virtually no interaction with other species, apart from that of predator and prey. Except for the lion, which will attack a leopard cub if it stumbles onto one without protection, the leopard has no predators. Other species give the leopard a wide berth.

The male leopard is larger than the female, growing up to 6 ft. long and weighing as much as 150 lbs. The female is normally about two-thirds the size of the male. Information on mating is largely drawn from zoos, since the leopard is so hard to observe in the wild. There is no particular breeding season; rather, the female appears in estrus, which lasts a few days, at intervals of three to seven weeks.

RIGHT: **THE LEOPARD'S SPOTTED COAT BLENDS EASILY INTO THE LIGHT AND SHADOWS OF THE TREE-STUDDED GRASSLANDS.** *OPPOSITE PAGE:* **A TREE PROVIDES A GOOD PLACE TO STORE A KILL FOR LATER MEALS, OUT OF SIGHT AND SMELLING RANGE OF OTHER PREDATORS.**

© Tom Mangelsen/Images of Nature

As with most other cats, mating is repeated frequently. The average litter is three cubs, which the mother keeps hidden until they are two months old. From this time, until they are full-size, they follow the mother. At about two years they are fully able to hunt. Even after the cubs can care for themselves and are not constantly with their mother, they may remain in contact for a time and greet each other affectionately, licking faces and rubbing bodies whenever they meet.

The spotted skin that is the leopard's camouflage also makes it a highly prized catch. The commerce in illegal furs, as well as the leopard's attacks on livestock, lead many to ignore the laws that protect it. Since 1972 the United States has banned the importation of leopard skins and articles made from them, but there is still an active market elsewhere. Several African governments have outlawed both hunting the leopard and all sales of leopard hides, but then look the other way while it continues. In Ethiopia, the slaughter of leopards over the past two decades has nearly decimated the population.

Chapter Five

Snow Leopard *Panthera uncia*

"This labyrinth of caves and ledges is a fine haunt for leopard, out of the way of its enemy, the wolf, and handy to a herd of bharal that is resident on the ridge above and often wanders down close to these cliffs. Perhaps, in the days left to us, we shall never see the snow leopard but it seems certain that the leopard will see us."

Peter Matthiessen, *The Snow Leopard*

The least known of all the big cats, the snow leopard (whose species name is *uncia*) not only lives in a forbidding, barely inhabited range, but carefully avoids contact with the few people who do live there. Researchers have spent months in areas they knew to be inhabited by this evasive cat, without catching even a glimpse of one.

At altitudes between 5,000 and 18,000 ft., the snow leopard's habitat covers the mountains of central Asia from northern Pakistan and Afghanistan, through Tibet to southwestern China, north into the Soviet Union and the Siberian border with Mongolia. Nowhere is it abundant; everywhere it is elusive.

Its habitat consists of craggy mountain slopes cut by deep gorges, mountain passes, and vast areas of frozen rock and snow just below the permanent snow line. Solitary cats hunt in territories that overlap the territories of others. Although they use the same paths and live close to one another, their shared areas are staggered in such a way that they seldom meet each other in their almost-constant patrolling in search of food

Although these territories are thought to be as large as thirty-five sq. mi., researchers Rodney Jackson and Darla Hibbard found their territories in the Langu Valley of western Nepal were no greater than twelve sq. mi.

The coat of the snow leopard is a frosty gray dotted with rosettes of black. These are blurred at the edges, their sharp contrast obscured in the heavy fur that protects the cat from the severe cold of the Himalayan winter. The average adult male is 4 to 5 ft. in length, with a heavily furred tail as long as 3 ft. In addition to providing balance for the cat as it leaps between rocky crags and along paths overhanging steep cliffs, the tail provides warmth, like a fur muffler, when the leopard rests.

The paws of the snow leopard are very large and its soles are covered with a thick cushion of hair to protect them from the cold and give a more even weight distribution when it walks on soft snow. Unlike its fellow members of the genus *Panthera*, the leopard does not roar, but researchers report its high-pitched yowling noises during the mating season.

THE SNOW LEOPARD'S COAT IS MARKED BY RINGS AND ROSETTES OF BLACK AGAINST A FROSTY GRAY BACKGROUND.

Kingdom:	Animalia	All animals
Phylum:	Chordata	Endo-skeletal animals with notochords
Subphylum:	Vertebrata	Animals with back-bones
Class:	Mammalia	Those with mammary glands and body hair
Order:	Carnivora	Those which feed mainly on meat
Suborder:	Fissipedia	Those whose feet have toes for land travel
Family:	Felidae	All cats
Genus:	*Panthera*	Those cats with carti-lage replacing the hyoid bone in the throat
Species:	*uncia*	Snow leopard

Very little is known of its social system, since even with radio signals they are hard to follow. Rodney Jackson explained in *National Geographic*, "They are easily concealed and we have spent many hours—the radio giving us a cat's exact location—looking in vain for a glimpse of sinuous tail or two revealing black flag ears."

Snow leopards hunt in the early morning, late afternoon, and evening, and may travel during midday as well. Unless they are caring for young or attending a kill, they are constantly on the move, settling into a new resting place each day. Since they are able to bring down prey much larger than themselves, a good kill may take a snow leopard a week to finish.

Mating season is between the months of January and March or April, with litters of one to four cubs born in June. The leopard hides her cubs in an inaccessible den high in the rocks protecting them from predators. The cubs develop quickly and are able to follow the mother along the rocky paths by the time they are a few months old. They remain with the mother for about two years before leaving to establish their own territories.

Snow leopards often stalk their prey in a low crouch, their colors blending into the rock because there is very little cover to hide behind. Their final lunge, sometimes from above their prey, may be over twenty ft. If the prey is fleeing, the leopard gives chase with long, powerful strides. The snow leopard's strength and tenacity allows it to kill prey over twice its own weight, sometimes clinging to the back of a sheep as it runs.

The favored prey of the snow leopard is the bharal, or blue sheep. It also eats tahr, ibex, markhor, musk deer, marmot, wild boar, mice, deer, birds, and hare. Its only predator is the wolf.

Study conditions are so difficult, and so much of the area virtually inaccessible (the Langu Gorge was not even mapped until 1964), that there is not even a rough estimate of the number of snow leopards

THE ROCKY TERRAIN OF THE HIMALAYAS PROVIDES LITTLE COVER, BUT THE SNOW LEOPARD IS STILL ABLE TO BLEND FAIRLY WELL INTO ITS SURROUNDINGS.

THE FEMALE SNOW
LEOPARD HIDES ITS CUBS
DEEP IN CAVES AND ROCKY
CREVICES AMONG THE
STEEP CLIFFS.

existing today. Nepal has created six mountain parks and reserves in areas where the snow leopard is known to live, but throughout the mountains of its range, populations are widely scattered, often fragmented into isolated groups without access to each other to strengthen the gene pool.

Villages exist in the reserves, and it is very difficult to change the habits of the mountain people who live here, who have traditionally killed the snow leopard because of its occasional raids on livestock. Hunting in these remote areas is almost impossible to control—only the timidity of the leopard saves it from hunters.

Snow leopard pelts, although banned from legal international trade, still demand quite a high price on the black market. In fact, snow leopard coats can be found in the government-run tourist stores of China.

In 1990, wildlife biologist Larry Barnes posed as a tourist interested in buying furs in Katmandu. He found thirty-one fur stores in that city selling coats made of furs from the snow leopard, clouded leopard, and other endangered cats. Shopkeepers even advised him on how to smuggle them into the United States.

A full length snow leopard coat requiring four adult animals costs $3,200 in Nepal and can be sold in Europe, the United States, or Japan for as much as $30,000. The skins are tanned and sewn in India, which, like Nepal, is a member of CITES. Both countries have laws prohibiting commerce in skins of endangered cats, but enforcement is nil and the coats are sold openly.

Fortunately, the wild population is not drained by illegal trade in live snow leopards. Snow leopards reproduce well in captivity and the supply of captive bred animals is ample.

Seeing the snow leopard in the wild is virtually impossible for the casual tourist, but on rare occasion a trek is offered by one of the specialty outfitters with the single purpose of seeking out the snow leopard's habitat. These are not regular offerings, however (see p. 114 for information on these outfitters).

Rodney Jackson, whose studies of the snow leopard in Nepal are quoted here, leads occasional treks especially designed to search for these elusive cats.

Chapter Six

Jaguar *Panthera onca*

"The chesty roar of jaguar in the night causes men to edge toward the blaze and draw serapes tighter. It silences the yapping dogs and starts the tethered horses milling. In announcing its mere presence in the blackness of night, the jaguar puts the animate world on edge."

Aldo Leopold, *Wildlife of Mexico*

The third largest of the cats, the jaguar is the only member of the genus *Panthera* to inhabit the Americas. From fossil evidence in North America, it is thought to have originated in the Old World, reaching North America from Asia and moving down through the isthmus into South America.

THE JAGUAR IS KNOWN AS "EL TIGRE" THROUGHOUT MOST OF ITS LATIN AMERICAN RANGE.

Amerigo Vespucci described "panthers" in Venezuela, using the term commonly applied to leopards in the fifteenth century. The untrained, casual observer might easily mistake the jaguar for a leopard, since their irregular black spots on a yellowish buff coat are similar. Vespucci is the earliest of the explorers to mention them.

The jaguar is larger than the leopard, its head broader, and its body more compact. The jaws of the jaguar are more powerful than those of the leopard, with well-developed teeth and jaw muscles that give the jaguar's bite its devastating power. In relation to its size, it is the strongest of any of the *Panthera* genus. From four to six ft. long, an adult male jaguar may weigh close to 250 lbs.

There are eight subspecies. The rarest of these are *P. o. hernandesi*, and *P. o. veracriucensis*, a few of which still survive in Mexico. The only Jaguar species found in the United States is the Arizona jaguar (*P. o. arizonensis*), found in Texas, Arizona, and northwest Mexico. The Yucatan jaguar (*P. o. goldmani*) is from the southwest Yucatan and Guatemala; the Panamanian jaguar (*P. o. centrais*) is found in Central America and Colombia; the Peruvian jaguar (*P. o. peruviana*) is found in Ecuador, Peru, and Bolivia. The Amazon jaguar (*P. o. onca*) is from the Orinoco and Amazon river basins; the Parana jaguar (*P. o. palustris*) is from Argentina and southern Brazil.

Like the leopard, the jaguar has proven to be quite adaptable to a variety of habitats, from low marshy jungles to elevations of nearly 9,000 ft. in Bolivia; from deep rain forests to open grasslands to desert. When dense forests or swamps thick with vegetation are available, the jaguar chooses these for a habitat, staying close to the riverine valleys.

Wherever the jaguar is found throughout Latin America, it is called *el tigre*, the Spanish word for tiger. The word jaguar is thought to derive from an old Indian name translating roughly to "wild animal that kills in one bound."

Kingdom:	Animalia	All animals
Phylum:	Chordata	Endo-skeletal animals with notochords
Subphylum:	Vertebrata	Animals with back-bones
Class:	Mammalia	Those with mammary glands and body hair
Order:	Carnivora	Those which feed mainly on meat
Suborder:	Fissipedia	Those whose feet have toes for land travel
Family:	Felidae	All cats
Genus:	*Panthera*	Those cats with cartilage replacing the hyoid bone in the throat
Species:	*onca*	Jaguar

As is the case with other cats, the markings on the face of each jaguar are so distinctive that those who work with them are able to distinguish one from another just as humans recognize friends when they meet them. They are much like fingerprint patterns in humans, with duplication very rare.

The folklore of the Maya and other peoples who inhabit the same range as the jaguar is filled with stories to explain a wide variety of natural phenomena, including how the jaguar got his spots. One version tells of a cub who ignored his mother's advice to be careful of humans. He challenged a woodcutter to a test of strength, and the woodcutter told him to put his paw into the split made by an ax in a piece of wood. While the jaguar's paw was in the split, the man removed the ax, leaving the paw fast in the wood as the split closed. Then he beat the jaguar with a stick, and to this day jaguars have bruised spots all over them.

In the Amazon forests, melanistic jaguars have been recorded; like the leopard, the faint pattern of slightly darker spots will show up in good light on these all-black animals. The Indians of the Amazon told explorer and naturalist Alexander von Humboldt that black jaguars were very rare, but in some places there are more black jaguars than spotted jaguars reported. Although there have been no studies on the subject (in fact, few on the jaguar at all), the Indians claim that black jaguars are, like the black leopard, the fiercest and most aggressive of the species.

There is an interesting difference, however, between the melanism of the jaguar and that of the leopard. While the trait in leopards results from a recessive gene, in jaguars it is a dominant gene. This, of course, leaves the question of what upsets the genetic makeup to prevent black jaguars from becoming more plentiful than the spotted. Somewhere, another genetic or adaptive trait is thought to prevent the dominant gene from prevailing.

Like other big cats, the jaguar can roar, but it is not known to do so. It grunts while hunting, occasionally cries out and growls when confronting what it perceives as danger, but does not roar in the commanding tones of the lion. During the mating season it has an almost mewing cry.

To date, there have been only two major scientific studies of the jaguar. The first was undertaken in 1983 in the rain forests of the Cockscomb Basin in southern Belize, under the sponsorship of the New York Zoological Society by zoologist Alan Rabinowitz. From 1988 to 1990, the government of Brazil, with the support of the National Geographic Society and the New York Zoological Society, sponsored a study in the Pantanal region. Both added tremendously to man's understanding of this reclusive animal and its habits. To effectively protect and save an animal, we must know how it lives, how much land it needs, what and how it eats, and how it relates to members of its own species as well as to others.

Both studies found the jaguar to be solitary and territorial. They move over areas whose sizes are determined primarily by the availability of prey; in Belize, these ranged from eleven to sixteen sq. mi. for males and about one-third of that territory for females. In both studies, territories were found to overlap considerably. When possible, the cats move along roads, trails, and waterways, with several using the same routes.

Although jaguars do considerable wandering within their territories, the boundaries are actively maintained by the resident males who seem to be readily recognized by others. They tolerate another moving through a portion of these occupied territories, but the interloper will not move into the home base of another. Within the large overall territories of each jaguar, they often stay in a small area—one sq. mi. or so—for as much as a week, until prey has been exhausted or alarmed into fleeing or hiding. Then in a single night the jaguar will move to another part of its territory and hunt there. The more dense the prey in an area, the smaller the jaguar's territory will be, and the longer it can stay at one base to hunt.

The activity pattern of individual jaguars seems to vary greatly, even within the same habitat. Although as opportunistic predators they may be active during any hour that food presents itself, they are usually nocturnal hunters. Most of their travel is after sunset and intermittently through the night. Most of the midday is spent resting, often on grassy beds, sometimes in trees.

The jaguar's ability to kill animals larger than itself allows it a wide variety of prey. This includes, where they are available, animals as large as the caiman and capybara. Armadillo, peccary, deer, monkeys, sloths, agouti, tapir, birds, and small rodents make up the bulk of their diet. Jaguars will eat turtles, which they scoop out of the shell without breaking it, as well as turtle eggs.

They also eat fish, and in the Amazon Basin Indians claim that jaguars fish by dangling their long tails in the water and moving them as

THE JAGUAR LIVES IN DENSE FOREST, MAKING IT VERY DIFFICULT TO STUDY AND SIGHT.

a lure. This story probably was started by people who observed the jaguar's tail in the water as it was fishing and assumed that since man used lures, so must the cat.

Patterns in the Belize study indicate that jaguars give birth to cubs between May and January, but most often between June and August. Births always occur during the rainy season when food and water are better distributed, so the mother does not have to travel far from the nest. No births in the wild were recorded during the February to May dry season.

One to four cubs are born to a litter and they remain with the mother for about two years before establishing territories of their own. In captivity the jaguar may live over twenty years, but in the wild, few make it past eleven due to parasites and hunting.

While the jaguar is considered vulnerable everywhere, and rare in the many parts of its range where its habitat has been destroyed or encroached upon by farming and lumbering, it is not classified as an endangered species. Hunting has been outlawed through most of its range, but enforcement is usually lax or nonexistent.

Alan Rabinowitz found it nearly impossible to convince the Mayans of southern Belize that they shouldn't kill jaguars and other cats at every encounter. Although no one had been harmed by one and there was no incident of jaguar attacking livestock, these Indians simply killed them by habit. The black market in illegal skins also encourages hunting, but Rabinowitz reports locals killing them and keeping the valuable skins just because they were "pretty."

During one twenty-one-month period, Rabinowitz documented ninety illegal jaguar kills, counting only those he knew about personally or could verify from reliable sources. In most places, such as Mexico, there is rarely even a token attempt to stop the hunting.

As the jaguar is actively hunted in some places and shot as a pest to livestock in others, its habitat continues to dwindle. In Brazil's Pantanal region, there are thought to be fewer than 1,000, and as the forests are cleared for farming, those jaguars whose territories are taken have begun to prey on the new animals that occupy it—the cattle. Farmers make no attempt to keep calves away from the forests where the jaguars wait; it is easier to lie in wait and kill the jaguar.

© A. Schmidecker/FPG International

The Mexican zoologist Miguel Alvarez del Toro told *National Geographic* reporter S. Jeffrey K. Wilkerson that "almost any animal whose habitat is the rain forests of Chiapas is now in danger of extinction."

The Mexican government, in an attempt to settle its remote areas, had transported families here to farm. The forests were cut or burned for a first-year crop of corn that exceeded a metric ton per hectare. But by the second year, the beating sun and the leeching rains made the thin layer of topsoil disappear, and the crop was less than 20 percent of the previous year's. Fields were abandoned and erosion turned them into a wasteland. Four hundred years of growth were traded for one year's crop.

JAGUAR CUBS REMAIN WITH THEIR MOTHER UNTIL THEY ARE ABOUT TWO YEARS OLD.

Logging continues, even in the reserves, with some 30 million board feet of lumber cut each year in the Lacandon region. Nearly twice that amount is used annually for cooking fires and home construction, while over 200 million board feet is burned or left to rot during land clearing. The jaguars hardly stand a chance.

Largely due to the efforts of Alan Rabinowitz, Belize declared the Cockscomb Basin the world's first jaguar preserve in 1984. The World Wildlife Fund has agreed to support this reserve, assuring, at least for a time, its maintenance.

But Belize is only one of the countries in the jaguar's range. International organizations have urged local governments to study the wildlife and have provided funds and experts to help them. Yet the forest environments continue to disappear at an alarming rate.

While there are a number of national parks in Central and South America that are well worth seeing, only one of these is dedicated to the jaguar. Even there, the chances of seeing one in the wild are thin—the jaguar is nocturnal, its habitat a deep jungle.

Visitors to Belize can go to the Cockscomb Basin Jaguar Preserve and learn about its work firsthand. While there, they can learn a lot about rain forests and their other denizens by visiting the replicated habitats of the Belize Zoo. The zoo occupies about 1,000 acres, and is a premier example of how zoos can educate people of all ages about the conservation of their vanishing resources.

The chances of seeing wild jaguars, even there, are limited by their habitat and nocturnal habits.

THE BELIZE ZOO IS A MAJOR FORCE IN EDUCATING LOCAL PEOPLE ON THE IMPORTANCE OF PRESERVING THE JAGUAR AND OTHER INDIGENOUS WILDLIFE.

Chapter Seven

Cheetah *Acinonyx jubatus*

"… The cubs chased each other around some doum palm saplings which gave them splendid cover for ambushing each other. How superbly their elegant movements fitted into the group of slender palms outlined against a brilliantly blue sky patterned with Kenya's almost permanent white clouds."

Joy Adamson (in *Pippa's Challenge*)

The sole member of its genus, the cheetah has many characteristics in common with the *Panthera*, but also many that separate it as well. The most noticeable difference is in its build, which is lighter, slimmer, and more streamlined than other big cats. Its legs are longer and its head is smaller, with a highly arched skull. The back is more flexible to allow greater speed, and the claws are not fully retractable as they are in other cats.

Joy Adamson, who raised a cheetah from a cub and returned it to the wild in a story much like that of her more famous lion Elsa, saw many similarities between cheetahs and dogs. In her book, *The Spotted Sphinx*, she describes these similarities: "Like a dog, it cannot retract its claws: it sits in doglike fashion and hunts like a canine; however, its pugmarks [tracks] are characteristic of a cat, as well as the use of the dewclaw and its possibly acquired ability to climb trees. Its sandy-colored coat is sleek like that of a short-haired dog, while its black spots are fluffy like a cat's fur."

Adamson also observed the retrieval instinct in cheetahs and noted that her cheetah, Pippa, was diagnosed as having *Babesia canis*, a tick-spread disease that affects dogs, whereas lions are subject to *Babesia felis*, a tick-spread disease that affects cats. The disease can be fatal.

The cheetah is thought to have separated from the other felids early in its evolution. Fossils from Europe and Asia, dating from the early Pleistocene (about 1 to 2 million years ago) show that these Ice Age animals were little different from the cheetah of today.

The name cheetah derives from *chita*, a Hindi word meaning "something that is spotted." Within recorded history the cheetah ranged throughout most of India, Afghanistan, Pakistan, and the Middle East, but the Asiatic subspecies, *A. j. venaticus*, is now virtually extinct. Although they had become rare by the end of the nineteenth century, it took until 1952 for India to ban the hunting of these cheetah—and that was only after the last three of these animals known to exist in India had been shot. A few still remain in Turkmenia, Kazakhstan, and Iran, all of which are strictly protected.

The African cheetah (*A. jubatus*) is found in open woodlands and savannahs from the Sudan south to the Eastern Transvaal and Namibia's Etosha Pan.

THE CHEETAH IS SMALLER, LIGHTER, AND NARROWER THAN OTHER BIG CAT SPECIES.

Kingdom:	Animalia	All animals
Phylum:	Chordata	Endo-skeletal animals with notochords
Subphylum:	Vertebrata	Animals with back-bones
Class:	Mammalia	Those with mammary glands and body hair
Other:	Carnivora	Those which feed mainly on meat
Suborder:	Fissipedia	Those whose feet have toes for land travel
Family:	Felidae	All cats
Genus:	*Acinonyx*	Distinguished by its looser build and smaller head
Species:	*jubatus*	Cheetah

The King cheetah (*A. j. rex*), first spotted in 1921 and found only in South Africa, was first thought to be a separate subspecies, but has been proven to be a product of a rare recessive gene. Some zoologists still maintain that it is a mutation, but the DeWildt Center, near Pretoria in South Africa, now breeds King cheetahs with the fifty-fifty result (two King, two not) necessary to prove the recessive gene. The spots of the King cheetah combine into a pattern of solid stripes along the back, and form small splotches on the body.

The most favorable habitat for the cheetah is in the savannahs, where there is a long dry spell during which grazing animals congregate near watering holes. Cheetahs do their best hunting in open areas where the grass is not too tall, because they depend upon the speed of their final dash to catch their prey. Thickly forested areas, or even heavy shrub growth, makes this straight sprint difficult.

Because of the timidity of the cheetah, it is uncertain whether they are territorial. It is generally agreed that they have certain territories and will avoid contact with others when their territories overlap. Since they roam over large areas as big as 300 sq. mi. the territories change, with some cheetahs occupying the territory at one time and others occupying it at another.

In places where grazing herds of gazelle migrate, so do the cheetahs that prey upon them. Female cheetahs travel farther to find prey than do males, whose established territories are also smaller.

Socially, the cheetah is solitary—especially the female. She is accompanied only by her cubs. Males sometimes form groups of two or three that remain together for long periods. When they are small,

THE HEAD OF THE CHEETAH IS QUITE SMALL IN RELATION TO ITS BODY, GIVING IT A STREAMLINED SHAPE HIGHLY SUITED TO RUNNING.

© Gerry Ellis/The Wildlife Collection

CHEETAH CUBS BEGIN TO HUNT AS YOUNG AS EIGHT MONTHS OLD, BUT TAKE SOME TIME TO BECOME EFFICIENT IN THEIR EFFORTS.

cubs play together, and their play is more related to the cheetah's adult behavior than is a lion cub's play. Stalking, chasing, and pouncing are characteristic—all skills that they will need to perfect for hunting. Even the swiping strike to the rear leg that brings the gazelle to the ground is imitated. Since the cubs follow the mother on hunts from a young age, it is not surprising that they should begin to repeat the actions that they see. Sometimes the snarling, pouncing cubs alert the prey that the mother is stalking. When the mother does succeed, the cubs are on the meat immediately, unlike the lion cubs who must wait for the adults to get their fill.

At about eight months the cubs begin joining actively in the hunt, although they are usually unsuccessful. They are inept and bumbling and the family's food supply may suffer seriously. But the teaching is an active effort on the mother's part; they have been observed to catch and hold small prey without injuring it, letting it go when the cubs are close enough to give chase. This might be repeated, with the mother holding and releasing a young gazelle several times for the cubs' practice, until they succeed.

By about the fifteenth to eighteenth month the cubs are ready to provide their own food and leave the mother, who usually mates soon thereafter. The cubs may remain together for a time before moving to different territories, and even then may occupy overlapping areas.

For centuries man has been puzzled by the fact that cheetahs, although easy to tame, do not breed easily in captivity. As far back as the seventeenth century, a Mogul emperor recorded having kept 1,000 cheetahs with only one litter born. Only rarely do they breed in zoos. George Schaller, who has studied all of the big cat species extensively, suggests that the cheetah's solitary existence in the wild may account for this. In zoos, the animals have more constant exposure to one another, which may throw off their natural pattern of mating. He suggests that the presence of a strange male may stimulate the female. The extensive research at the DeWildt Center seems to bear out this theory. This may be an adaptive behavior that maintains variability in the gene pool of a species, which is usually fairly sparsely spread in any area.

The cheetah is more diurnal than other cats, hunting later into the morning and earlier in the afternoon than other cats. During the hottest part of the day the cheetah sleeps or rests. The cheetah usually sleeps at night, although it will hunt by moonlight.

Because the cheetah's habitat is the same as larger carnivores, including the lion and the leopard, it must adapt to enable it to use the same resources in different ways so as to avoid competition and encounters that it could not win. Thus, the cheetah hunts at different hours than its competition and depends upon its speed and stealth to compensate for its comparative lack of strength and size.

The cheetah is the fastest of all land animals, capable of speeds of up to sixty mph for short durations. Its claws do not retract, providing greater traction as it runs. By moving as close as possible to a grazing herd under cover of tall grass, the cheetah minimizes the energy that it will expend in the final chase.

When the cheetah reaches its prey, it slaps at the hind legs (or forelegs of larger animals), usually bringing the animal to the ground. The cheetah is not as strong as larger cats and has adapted to compensate for this, too, with a swift, sure-kill method. Because the roots of its teeth are relatively small, the nasal passage remains open while the teeth are tightly clamped, allowing the cheetah to hold onto a victim's throat in a steady bite for several minutes. By this time the chase has used up so much of the victim's oxygen supply that it cannot struggle as its windpipe is closed off and it suffocates.

Several observers have seen a cheetah abandon a hunt if the gazelle does not run. On the rare occasion when one stands its

ground, the cheetah moves off to other prey, presumably because a gazelle that has not been chased and would not be tired could be able either to struggle loose, or would not suffocate in a short enough time. Because of the length and speed of the chase, the cheetah does not need the jaw and shoulder strength (hence the bulk and the weight) of the other big cats. This allows for a streamlined build, which in turn allows for the higher speed produced by the cheetah.

One problem that the cheetah has with daylight kills is the probability of being spotted by vultures, which can drive a cheetah from a kill or advertise it to an opportunistic lion who will appropriate the meal. The cheetah therefore drags the prey to cover before eating.

THE CHEETAH DEPENDS ON A LONG CHASE TO TIRE ITS PREY SUFFICIENTLY AND MAKE SUFFOCATION QUICK.

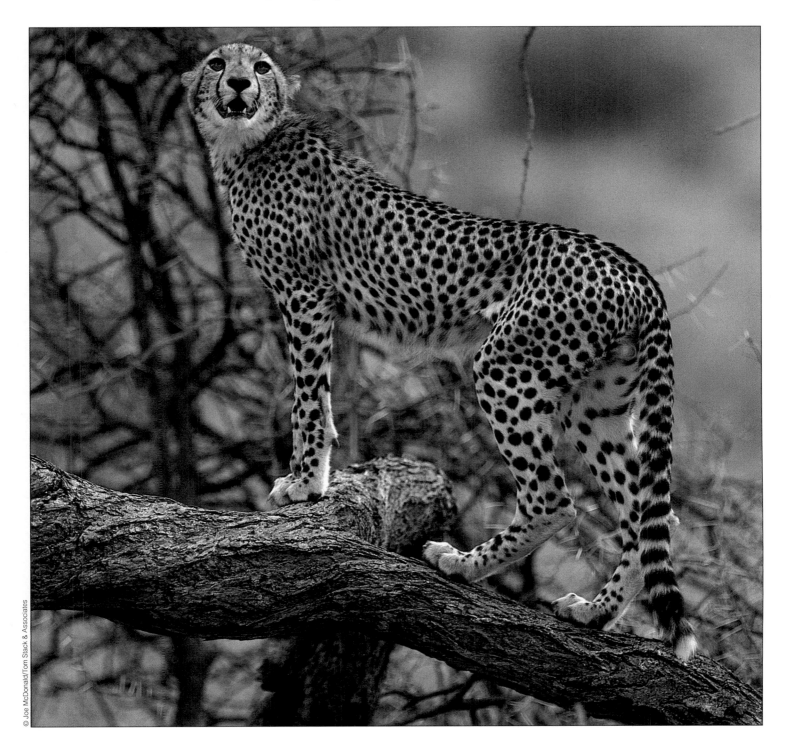

THE CHEETAH IS A VERY SECRETIVE AND PROTECTIVE MOTHER, MOVING CUBS OFTEN TO KEEP PREDATORS FROM CATCHING THEIR SCENT.

The cheetah eats rapidly until it is full, then abandons the kill. Unlike other big cats, the cheetah never returns to the remains and will not eat meat that has not been freshly killed. This is a luxury that the cheetah can afford, since it is a more efficient hunter than the lion or the leopard, with a high percentage of its chases ending in a kill.

The gazelle is the preferred prey of the cheetah in the Serengeti-Masai Mara region, and the common impala is the cheetah's most important food source in Kruger National Park. The cheetah is capable of bringing down young giraffe, buffalo, zebra, and wildebeest, and will occasionally prey upon other smaller animals such as jackal, aardvark, and hare.

When chasing larger animals such as wildebeest, the cheetah's tactic is to rush the herd and cause panic. As the wildebeest flee, the cheetah identifies a calf and tries to separate it from the rest of the herd during the confusion. With the calf unprotected by its mother, the cheetah can bring it down quickly and drag it to cover before its mother can find it.

The cheetah is at the bottom of the large predator hierarchy. Lions, leopards, and hyena not only will take downed prey from the cheetah but also prey on cheetah cubs as well. Only the jackal is lower on the predation scale.

The cheetah has no single breeding season and cubs are born in all months. When the female is in estrus she advertises this by her scent, to which males, through whose territories she is passing, are attracted.

It is hard to study cheetah cubs in the wild during their first few weeks, since the mother is very secretive. Litter sizes seem to vary between one and nine but the mortality rate is high during the first weeks and remains high until the cubs are about four months old. Although studies have differed in their findings, overall cub mortality is estimated to be between 50 and 75 percent. To hide the cubs from the noses of predators, the mother frequently moves them to a clean spot, usually well covered with underbrush. By the time they are five or six weeks old the cubs begin to follow their mother as she hunts.

If all of the cubs in a litter die, the mother immediately comes into estrus and conceives another litter, even if she is not fully recovered from the birth of the first litter.

THE CHEETAH CUB IS PREY TO LION, LEOPARD, AND HYENA.

Although the cheetah is not plentiful anywhere, its population seems to have stabilized within the past decade and it has been removed from the endangered species list. It is now designated as rare. Because its environmental needs put it in the same habitats as larger predators, its numbers will never be tremendous, but those parks with cheetah populations have distributions that remain fairly constant.

The cheetah's low place on the predator scale means that it is the first to feel the scarcity of game. In areas like the Masai Mara and Serengeti, where the vicissitudes of climate and diseases such as rinderpest cause natural variations of game populations, it is foreseeable that the great herds of wildebeest, gazelle, and other grazers will ebb,

OPPOSITE PAGE: **THE CHEETAH IS EASILY DISTINGUISHED BY ITS SMALL SIZE, NARROW BUILD, AND THE "TEAR LINES" BELOW ITS EYES.** *BELOW:* **IT IS UNUSUAL TO SEE ADULT CHEETAHS IN GROUPS, BUT A LITTER OF SUB-ADULTS WILL REMAIN TOGETHER.**

as they have done in the past. When, and if, this happens, the cheetah will be the first to suffer. Larger predators will get "the lion's share" of what is available.

Efforts to reintroduce the cheetah into areas where it has declined or disappeared entirely have not always been successful, especially if lions already live there. Studies and controlled experiments by the DeWildt Center have already yielded helpful information and will continue to suggest ways to protect and preserve the cheetah.

In the more arid zones of Africa—the Sahel and the Kalahari—the cheetah has managed well. Because the cheetah needs less water

© Gerry Ellis/The Wildlife Collection

THE CHEETAH NEEDS LESS WATER THAN OTHER CATS AND CAN SURVIVE IN THE GRASSLANDS OF ARID REGIONS.

than the larger predators, it can survive in these areas. Smaller, it can hunt successfully in shorter grasses. The nature of these places makes them unsuited to settlement by man. These habitats are the least subject to any encroachment that would limit the cheetah's range.

Unfortunately, the lion population at Etosha National Park in Namibia has increased and old migratory routes have been fenced. Anthrax has depleted the wildebeest herd, forcing the lion to rely more heavily on springbok, formerly the cheetah's main food source there; thus the cheetah population is declining. To reverse this, the old migratory routes should be reopened to reestablish the natural flow of populations, but the newly independent Namibia has problems that supercede any efforts to preserve wildlife.

Under the influence of South Africa, they had access to wildlife management expertise as well as the clout of a very conservation-minded government. The future of the cheetah and other wildlife may not be the first concern of the new government in Namibia, but it is a hopeful sign that they have sought the help of the South African Rangers in controlling poachers.

© Gerry Ellis/The Wildlife Collection

The cheetah's pelt is not a preferred fur source, but poaching for skins still continues. Fortunately for the cheetah, it has little taste for any but freshly killed meat, so luring one to traps is not easy. Timidity works in the cheetah's favor, too. The cheetah is not a major threat to livestock and is rarely seen near human habitation, so farmers and herdsmen do not hunt it to protect stock. As with other animals, its greatest threat is from encroachment on its habitat by farms and fences, which limit the availability of its food sources.

THE TIMID CHEETAH SELDOM VENTURES INTO INHABITED AREAS IN SEARCH OF LIVESTOCK OR DOGS.

THE CHEETAH HUNTS LATER IN THE MORNING AND BEGINS EARLIER IN THE EVENING, INCREASING THE CHANCES OF DAYLIGHT SIGHTINGS BY SAFARI-GOERS.

For the same reason that cheetahs are difficult for scientists to study in the wild, they are a hard quarry for visitors to their habitats to spot. Unlike the leopard, the cheetah has no favored perch in an acacia tree, and unlike the lion they do not stretch out confidently in the open to rest. The cheetah's movements are often furtive and usually under cover. It takes sharp eyes and a ranger who knows the area well to find one.

On the traveler's side, however, is the cheetah's diurnal nature. It moves more during daylight hours, and is active later in the morning and earlier in the evening. Water holes are not as good for attracting cheetah, since they can go for days without a drink.

The cheetahs of the Serengeti are hard to spot because the game drives are usually between lodges, with drivers from Arusha who are neither well trained in wildlife habits nor familiar with local wildlife patterns. All vehicles must stay on the roads here, so it is difficult to find and follow the cheetah. Chances are best during the dry season, July through March.

In Kruger Park, the best place to look for cheetahs is in the low, open veld areas. Rangers and trackers in the private reserves of the Sabie Sand are well trained and very familiar with the area and its animals and may be more successful in spotting one. Small groups and off-road driving increase the likelihood of seeing cheetah. While in the area, those especially interested in cheetahs should visit the DeWildt Center for a tour conducted by their staff. This provides a rare chance to see the King cheetah.

The Kenya parks where cheetah are seen most often are Amboseli, Masai Mara, Tsavo, and Samburu—especially the latter two. Samburu is unlike other East African parks in that its habitat is semiarid and well isolated. Both here and at Tsavo it is critical to have a guide who knows animal habits and the terrain well and who is willing to look for specific species, not just make an obligatory run through the most commonly traveled and least difficult route. It is also helpful to tell the ranger what species of big cats are of particular interest to you, since they so often deal with visitors whose sole interest is limited to viewing the "big five" game animals. (See appendix for outfitters in these areas.)

Travel Sources

Since the remaining wild habitats for big cats are usually in remote places where travel is difficult, the choice of an outfitter is very important. While any travel agent can book clients on an African safari, most are not in a position to know which of these safaris offer the serious traveler an in-depth look at environments. Cost is not always a clue, since extra expense may be for luxury lodges, when a tented bush camp would offer a better wildlife experience. Trips to destinations outside the standard safari itineraries are often difficult to find.

When planning any wildlife or environmental trip it is best to work directly with the outfitter. Their expertise is based on a thorough knowledge of the place and you should be discussing your trip with someone who has actually been to the places you will be going. Expect this kind of first-hand experience from your outfitter and go elsewhere if you don't find it.

The following travel consultants, outfitters, and sources of information specialize in environmental explorations, treks, and safaris. They offer reliable information on destinations and types of trips that are difficult to book elsewhere. With them are listed the specific destinations mentioned in this book.

A World Apart
P.O. Box 44207
Nairobi, Kenya
Fax 254-2-333262
Telex 22526
(May also be booked through Classic Tours, below.)

Luxury tented safaris in Kenya and Tanzania, including Masai Mara, Samburu, the Mount Kenya area, the Serengeti, and camping on the floor of the Ngorongoro Crater.

Classic Tours International
625 North Michigan Avenue
Chicago, Illinois 60611

Safaris of all varieties in Kenya and Tanzania, including the Serengeti, Masai Mara, Tsavo, Amboiseli, Samburu, Tarangire, Lake Manyara, Aberdare, and the Ngorongoro Crater. Also safaris in Botswana to the Okavango Delta and Chobe.

Far Horizons Cultural Discovery Trips
P.O. Box 1529
16 Fern Lane
San Anselmo, CA 94960

Nature and cultural trips to Belize, including the Cockscomb Basin and the Belize Tropical Education Center.

Flamingo Tours of Africa
139A New Bond Street
London W1Y 9FB, England

Kenya and Tanzania safaris including the Masai Mara, Serengeti, Ngorongoro Crater, Samburu, Tsavo, Mt. Kenya parks, Aberdares, Amboiseli, and Tarangire.

InnerAsia Expeditions
2627 Lombard Street
San Francisco, CA 94123

Nepal and India, including a snow leopard trek led by Rodney Jackson, elephant-back safaris in the Chitwan Reserve, and trips to Ranthambhor Reserve; also trips to the Siberian Tiger reserves in Manchuria and Siberia, and the Bandhavgarh Jungle Camp for tiger viewing.

International Expeditions
1776 Independence Court
Birmingham, AL 35216

Belize naturalist tours including Cockscomb Basin Jaguar Reserve; trips to Rathambhor in India.

Ker Downey Selby
13201 Northwest Freeway
Houston, Texas 77040

Botswana, including fly-in safaris to the Okavango Delta and Chobe.

Mountain Travel
6420 Fairmount Avenue
El Cerrito, California 94530

Group camping safaris in Kenya and Tanzania; tours to Ranthambhor and Dudhwa National Park in India.

SATOUR
747 Third Avenue
New York, New York 10017
or
Suite 1001 20 Elgin Avenue West
Toronto, Ontario MR4 1K8
Canada

Information on safaris in Southern Africa, including Inyati, Mala Mala, Kruger Park, Etosha Pan, DeWildt Center, Sabie Sand reserves, and Botswana.

Solrep International
2524 Nottingham
Houston, Texas 77005

Southern Africa safaris to Etosha, Kruger Park, and Sabie Sand reserves.

Sporting International
14 Old Bond Street
London W1X 3DB, England
Fax 01-491-9177

Fly-in safaris to the Okavango Delta and Chobe in Botswana as well as other parks in Southern Africa.

Tropical Travel
720 Worthshire
Houston, TX 77008

Belize nature and cultural tours including the Cockscomb Basin Jaguar Reserve.

Suggested Reading

Adamson, George. *My Pride and Joy*, NY: Simon and Schuster, 1987.

Adamson, Joy. *Born Free*, NY: Pantheon, 1960.

Pippa's Challenge, NY: Balantine Books, 1972.

The Spotted Sphinx, NY: Harcourt Brace, 1969.

Amman, Katherine and Karl. *Cheetah*, NY: Arco, 1985.

Gartelmann, Karl Deiter. *Digging Up Prehistory*, Quito, Ecuador: Ediciones Libri Mundi, 1986.

Hallet, Jean-Pierre. *Animal Kitabu*, NY: Random House, 1968.

Congo Kitabu, NY: Random House, 1965.

Kingsley, Mary. *Travels in West Africa*, London: Macmillan, 1897.

Koch-Isenburg, Ludwig. *The Realm of the Green Buddha*, NY: Viking, 1963.

Leopold, Aldo S. *Wildlife of Mexico*, Berkeley: University of California Press, 1959.

Macdonald, David, ed. *The Encyclopedia of Mammals*, NY: Facts on File, 1984.

Matthiessen, Peter. *The Snow Leopard*, NY: Viking, 1978.

McFarland, David, ed. *The Oxford Companion to Animal Behavior*, NY: Oxford University Press, 1982.

McNeely, Jeffrey A. and Paul Spencer Wachtel. *The Soul of the Tiger: Searching for Nature's Answers in Exotic Southeast Asia*, NY: Doubleday, 1988.

Moorhead, Alan. *No Room in the Ark*, NY: Harper and Brothers, 1957.

Palmer, Eve. *The Plains of Camdeboo*, NY: Viking, 1967.

Patterson, J. H. *The Man Eaters of Tsavo*, NY: St. Martin's, 1985.

Rabinowitz, Alan. *Jaguar: Struggles and Triumphs in the Jungles of Belize*, NY: Arbor House, 1986.

Schaller, George B. *The Deer and the Tiger*, Chicago: University of Chicago Press, 1967.
    Golden Shadows, Flying Hooves, NY: Alfred Knopf, 1973.
    The Serengeti Lion, Chicago: University of Chicago Press, 1972.

Thapar, Valmik. *Tiger: Portrait of a Predator*, NY: Facts on File, 1986.

Periodicals

Barnes, Larry. "Nepal: Endangered Cats Victims of Illegal Fur Market." *Wildlife Conservation* (July/August 1990).

Bartlett, Des and Jen. "Family Life of the Lions." *National Geographic* (December 1982).

Breedan, Stanley and Belinda Wright. "Tiger! Lord of the Indian Jungle." *National Geographic* (December 1984).

Chadwick, Douglas H. "Etosha: Namibia's Kingdom of Animals." *National Geographic* (March 1983).

Drucker, Phillip and Robert F. Heizer. "Gifts for the Jaguar God." *National Geographic* (September 1976).

Jackson, Rodney and Dana Hillard. "Tracking the Snow Leopard." *National Geographic* (January 1986).

Putnam, John J. "India Struggles to Save Her Wildlife." *National Geographic* (September 1976).

Schaller, George. "The Wilderness of the World Lives in the Heart of the Tiger." *International Wildlife* (November/December 1973).

Conservation Organizations

World Wildlife Fund
1250 24th St., NW
Washington, D.C. 20037

International Union for Conservation of
Nature (IUCN)
Avenue du Mont-Blanc
CH-1196 Gland
Switzerland

Wildlife Conservation International
New York Zoological Society
185th St. and Southern Blvd.
Bronx, NY 10460

Project Tiger
Sawai Madhopur
Rajasthan India

Index